The Influence of Religious Beliefs on Social Interaction

AF763642

European University Studies
Europäische Hochschulschriften
Publications Universitaires Européennes

Series XXII
Sociology

Reihe XXII Série XXII
Soziologie
Sociologie

Vol./Bd. 396

PETER LANG
Frankfurt am Main · Berlin · Bern · Bruxelles · New York · Oxford · Wien

Yongling Xue

The Influence of Religious Beliefs on Social Interaction

PETER LANG
Europäischer Verlag der Wissenschaften

Bibliographic Information published by Die Deutsche Bibliothek
Die Deutsche Bibliothek lists this publication in the Deutsche Nationalbibliografie; detailed bibliographic data is available in the internet at <http://dnb.ddb.de>.

Zugl.: München, Univ., Diss., 2004

D 19
ISSN 0721-3379
ISBN 3-631-52614-8
US-ISBN 0-8204-7311-1

© Peter Lang GmbH
Europäischer Verlag der Wissenschaften
Frankfurt am Main 2004
All rights reserved.

All parts of this publication are protected by copyright. Any utilisation outside the strict limits of the copyright law, without the permission of the publisher, is forbidden and liable to prosecution. This applies in particular to reproductions, translations, microfilming, and storage and processing in electronic retrieval systems.

www.peterlang.de

Preface

Ms. Xue divides her text into six chapters. In the introduction she presents the concept of reality in the continuity of Peter L. Berger and Thomas Luckmánn which she intends to follow throughout her dissertation. In chapter 2 she explains the topic in detail and outlines the theoretical background. It is her goal in this analysis to stay as close a possible to the notion of religion which the persons she interviews have themselves in their everyday experience, and then to find out how those who define themselves as "religious" differ in their interaction with their fellow humans from those who consider themselves "not religious". In addition she strives in chapter 2 to clarify the terminology and to introduce some aspects of role theory. Following the ideas of George H. Mead and Eving Goffman she asks if certain aspects of interaction theory can be applied to dealing with persons in the beyond or "immortals".

In chapter 3 the author explains her research method. She decides to use a combination of quantitative and qualitative procedure and introduces her questionnaire, the guideline for the interviews, and the sampling technique. The data were gathered since the end of December 2002 and are therefore quite up to date. She describes the process of collecting and analysing the data which came from an almost equal number of Germans and Chinese (living in Munich, Germany). She also succeeded in keeping the number of "religious" and of "not religious" respondents well balanced within each national group. Her questionnaire reached 209 persons. Thus she presents her data in four subgroups of about 50 cases each. In addition there were 32 in depth interviews to supply the qualitative component of her analysis. Again, there are Germans and Chinese and within each of those "religious" versus "not religious" respondents, and accordingly there are about 8 cases in each group.

In chapter 4 Ms. Xue presents the data from the questionnaire. It is interesting to see how well balanced the data are not only by attitude toward religion – which indeed was the main purpose of the study – but also by nationality, sex, age etc. in spite of the simple sampling technique of the author. Of course the proportion of married people is twice as high among the Chinese (60%) than among the Germans (about 30%), but that is not an artifact of the study but an indication of differences in national culture.

Another notional difference turns up in the replies to the question about the deceased relatives: Not quite half (47%) of the "religious" Germans, but almost 60% of the "religious" Chinese assume that those continue to exist in a remote place, while 58% of the Germans and 55% of the Chinese consider their lives deleted. A majority of all four groups keeps the memory of the dead loved ones alive, but as many as 10,6% of the German "religious" and even 13,6% of the Chinese "religious" think that they have had a real encounter with a deceased family member after that person died!

Ms. Xue appends "small summaries" to each chapter. In chapter 5 she presents the results of her in depth interviews. She quotes detailed passages from the taperecorded dialogues. This leads to important added information which enables her to interpret the questionnaire data with more clarity and reliability. She distinguishes (in the questionnaire as well as in the interviews) between two types of interaction: with wellknown partners or with strangers, and if with strangers, whether the encounter occurs in a familiar or in an unfamiliar setting. The striking result is that hardly any differences can be found between "religious" and "not religious" respondents in their interactions with their contemporaries, although in each of the two groups they may be guided by different types of motivation.

The final chapter 6 presents „discussion and conclusion“ as a review of what has been achieved in the study. The author creates her own typology of interpretations of death among “religious” versus “not religious” persons, an outline for how to relate to dead ancestors and to offspring, and a comparison between images of god (or gods) in western religion versus eastern religions. It deserves recognition that Ms. Xue has completed her research in Germany in a social environment where she has no command of the native language, that she worked more or less on her own and without any research budget, and that nevertheless she came up with insights some of which are indeed surprising. The literature on the sociology of religions since the “classics” is burdened with a western bias. Therefore too it is useful if a woman from mainland China who grew up without any exposure to religion, approaches here old questions from a fresh perspective.

München, Germany, February 20, 2004

Horst J. Helle

Contents

Acknowledgments

To use sincere words expressing my heartfelt thankfulness:

I am thankful to my first supervisor Professor Dr. Horst Helle and my second supervisor Privatdozent Dr. Ludwig Nieder for directing me writing the dissertation!

I am thankful to Deutscher Akademischer Austauschdienst and Hanns-Seidel-Stiftung for the financial support in my last phase of the doctoral study!

I am thankful to all the friends for helping me during the process of work, especially to those who helped me rolling the snowball in the survey!

I am thankful to my parents for bringing me up and setting good examples for me in academic research!

Chapter 1: Introduction

1. Social Reality in the World

Using our own eyes to observe the world, colourful lives and varied people can be seen. Life is colourful because it is created by varied people. People are varied because they are influenced by colourful lives. It is a phenomenon which exists objectively and subjectively recognized. It exists objectively even when it is independent of our own volition. It is subjectively recognized though the same thing may be endowed with different meanings by different people. It is what we called social reality (Berger and Luckmann 1973: pp.13-48).

Social reality is different from the reality which is usually referred in natural sciences. It should not be thought of as just a thing which exists objectively out there. It is something that human beings constantly negotiate and recreate (Karp 1986: p.50). It is a process, according to Peter Berger (Berger 1969: pp.3-52), of the ongoing outpouring of human beings into the world, both in the physical and the mental activity of man (externalization), of the attainment by the products of the activity of a reality as a facticity external to (objectivation), of the reappropriation by man of the same reality transforming it from the objective world into the subjective consciousness (internalization). It is through externalization that society is a human product. It is through objectivation that socicty becomes a reality. It is through internalization that man is a product of society. That is the reality being taken as the object of the analyses in sociology.

2. Experiencing Social Reality in Everyday Life

Social reality presents itself in the form of everyday life (Berger and Luckmann 1973: pp.13-48). We can suppose the typical life of a professional husband and his housekeeper wife a day in traditional society. They got up in the morning, the husband had breakfast in a hurry which was prepared by his wife. The husband went to work during the daytime while his wife did housework and took care of children at home (or went to her neighbours chatting sometimes). The husband came back home in the evening and his wife made supper for him. After supper, they enjoyed leisure time together, then went to sleep......The life went on day after day quietly. They might seldom think about it and took it for granted. Everybody lived the same way and there were few exceptions.

But, the quiet life did not last too long. One day, just from that day, the wife said to the husband and insisted on saying from then on: I want to go to work outside the home. The words which are so common nowadays might have surprised the husband a lot at that time. Maybe the wife was one of the first few who were the pioneers of the statement. Maybe there were many in front of her who influenced her. But this is not important. What is important is that the women wanted to work outside becoming a reality, a reality of everyday life or a life which is different from the reality of everyday in the past. Did the husband recognize the reality? How did he interpret it? What would he react to it? Concerning these questions, a dialogue would be set off between the husband and wife. The dialogue is what we called in sociology a form of social interaction. Therefore, to recognize and to experience the existence of the social reality is in everyday life, to be more exact, in the process of social interaction.

To analyse the example above we can see some characteristics of social reality. The reality of everyday life appears as an ordered reality. It is objectively existed. The husband and wife lived in a place that geographically located. The reality of everyday life is organized around the place where the people are and the time when people present. It can be subjectively experienced, for instance, the office where the husband worked and the home where the wife kept. The reality of everyday life presents itself as an intersubjective world which one shares with others. It refers to a world that is common to many people. The husband and wife understood each other and interacted with each other. The reality of everyday life does not require proof. It is simply there and known as real. The husband might feel doubt about what the wife said but he was obliged to suspend such doubt as he routinely existed in everyday life (Berger and Luckmann 1973: pp.13-48).

Why might the husband feel doubt about what the wife said? Because everybody has socially recognized positions in a social system (status) with certain expectations about what one will do and will not do (role). Husband and wife are not expected to act in the same way in different societies (Kammeger, Ritzer and Yetman 1997: pp.93-95). In traditional society, only men were expected to work hard, while women were expected to be thrifty in managing a household. Just like the players on the stage, for the actors of society, their interaction is to be viewed as structured by the script, director, other actors and the audience, such as the expectations of them. At the same time, their interaction is also to be seen as influenced by the wide range of tactics available to participants, such as the dialogue between actors (Turner 1991: p.410).

3. Experiencing Social Reality in Sacred Cosmos

Compared to the reality of everyday life, social reality also presents itself in the form of a sacred cosmos (Berger and Luckmann 1973: pp.13-48, Berger 1969: pp.3-52). The sacred cosmos is confronted by man as an immensely powerful reality other than man's self. This reality addresses itself to man and locates man's life in an ultimately meaningful order. People sometimes recognize that they are living in the two kinds of realities, moving back and forth between the two of them. The vivid metaphors of this experience are, for example, moving between the reality of a dream and the reality of everyday life or moving between the world of everyday life and the world of play (Berger and Luckmann 1973: 13-48). A person may dream that he drives a car to Rome, while waking up from the dream, he has to take the U-Bahn to work. A person may see a terrible fight going on as the curtain rises of a play, while as the curtain falls, he finds that he is surrounded by friendly people. Conversely, an exhausted worker is so eager to have a vacation that he may dream that he takes a trip to Rome. A despaired woman in her broken up marriage may have the experience that when she is praying before the Buddha, a powerful voice spread from somewhere from the beyond: Comply with luck! Be tolerant!

Many examples can be made. It is obvious that the two kinds of realities are different. The reality of a dream is different from the reality of everyday life. The reality in the world of everyday life is different from the reality in the world of play. It is important. But what is more important is that people with different views of the world may deal with the realities differently. How do people deal with the reality of a dream and the reality of a play? What happened in the dream or in the play is truth or false? Is it a reality or fantasy? If the person believes that the trip to Rome in the dream is truth, he may "feel relaxed" after the dream otherwise he may feel more exhausted; If the person believes that the voice from the beyond is truth, she may "talk to the one" from the beyond and become tolerant otherwise she may feel more despaired.

4. Religious Beliefs and Social Interaction

In everyday life, a person may interact with a wide variety of people, the people in the street (strangers), the people in the family (intimates), or the people in the beyond (like the one in the example above). As long as people can share the same idea (symbol), the idea which express the common meaning of the people and which can be understood by both sides of communication, all kinds of situations can be negotiated and recreated. Human beings with the abilities to understand and use symbols, both verbal and nonverbal, make interaction possible (Kammeger, Ritzer and Yetman 1997: pp.91-92). People interact not only with others but with themselves. That is how we differentiate between covert behaviour and overt behaviour. Covert behaviour is the thinking process while overt behaviour is the actual behaviour performed by an actor. Most human action involves both kinds (Ritzer 1992: pp.351-352). To analyse people in social interaction, we need to analyse not only the overt behaviour but also the covert behaviour behind the overt.

The interaction among human beings is realised in empirical action. The interaction between human beings and the beyond is, in fact, a belief, or a personal experience derived from the belief. The relationship between the two kinds of interaction is that of the relationship between beliefs and actions. It is the topic of this dissertation: The Influence of Religious Beliefs on Social Interaction. It is assumed that religious beliefs play an important role in social interaction. What are the differences in social interaction between those who have religious beliefs and those who do not have religious beliefs: how do they associate with others? why do they associate with others that way? how do they interpret problems? what do they usually do according to their interpretation? The purpose of the research is: (1) to have a better understanding of the concept of religion; (2) to explore the function of religion in everyday life.

Religious beliefs come in many kinds. For example: the belief in spirit which means to believe in the existence of a supernatural thing that is inside the body of the individual, giving life to the individual and dominating all activities of the individual; the belief in God which means to believe in a supernatural being which has power over nature and control of human affairs. God has abilities to dominate and manipulate nature and human beings. God can create some special events or miracles according to his will (Lu Daji 1998: pp.104-258). In this research, the focus will be the beliefs in spirit or God, whatever, to be more exact, the presence of immortals in the beyond.

Social interaction occurs in many forms as well. According to the subjects of interaction, it can be divided into the interaction between individuals and the interaction between groups. According to the forms of interaction, it can be divided into the interaction conducted face to face or by the way of media and agents. According to the nature of interaction, it can be divided into competition and cooperation (Han Mingmo 1993: pp.55-61). Moreover, considering the communication between human beings and the beyond, it can be divided into the interaction with the presence of immortals and the interaction with the absence of immortals. In this research, it will concentrate on the interaction between individuals by the way of face to face contact, to be more exact, the interaction between strangers (biographical strangers and cultural strangers) and between the intimates (relatives and lovers) in the situation of the presence or absence of immortals in the beyond.

5. The Structure of the Dissertation

The dissertation is divided into six chapters. Chapter one is a general introduction to introduce the background of the research and to put forward the theme of the dissertation. Chapter two is a theoretical framework to review and discuss previous research and theories concerning with the themes and to raise questions and assumptions on the research. Chapter three is research design to introduce the survey method of the research including the sample of the research, operational concepts and assumptions, the process of data collection, and the method of data analysis. Chapter four gives the results from the questionnaire. It is a description of the people, their beliefs and their interaction. Chapter five gives the results from the interview. It is compatible with the results from the questionnaire. It is an explanation of the people. Some representative examples are made in order to reveal the inner world of the people and to have a better understanding of them. Chapter six is the discussion and the conclusion to discuss and analyse the results from the questionnaire and the interview and to express a general opinion on the discussion and the analysis.

Chapter 2: Theoretical Framework

1. The Theme of the Dissertation

Previous approaches on social reality provide an outlook for social studies. It is that social reality does not only present itself in the form of everyday life but also present itself in the form of sacred cosmos. Previous theories on social interaction provide a framework for later research. It is that social interaction goes on under a certain structure and varies in its process. It means that social interaction has a structured form although its contents might be varied in its process (to apply the dialectical relationship between form and content by Georg Simmel). Using Jonathan Turner's analogy of a play and a game to illustrate the relationship between the structured form and varied contents, we may say that there are varied games in a patterned play. In fact, a game also has its rules. A game can be conversely viewed as a form of a play. The differences between a play and a game are derived from the angle of the viewers. When human action is seen as occurring in a theatre, interaction is likely to be viewed as a play. When human action is conceptualized as a game, interaction is likely to be seen as influenced by the wide range of tactics available to participants.

The title of the dissertation is "The Influence of Religious Beliefs on Social Interaction". It is supposed that religious beliefs play an important role in social interaction. What are the differences between those who have religious beliefs and those who do not have religious beliefs when associating with people and dealing with problems in everyday life: how do they interpret others and the problems? what do they usually do in relation to the interpretation? This is the theme of the dissertation. The purpose of the research is: (1) to have a better understanding of the concept of religion; (2) to explore the function of religion in everyday life. The research contains the following assumptions: (1) to assume that people who have religious beliefs may have something in common in social interaction; (2) to assume that people who have religious beliefs may have something different from the people who do not have religious beliefs in social interaction; (3) to assume that it is possible that in reality the facts may contradict the first two assumptions.

1.1 The Common Characteristics Of the Religious Believers in Social Interaction

On the basis of the structural role theory, it is assumed that people who have religious beliefs may have something in common in social interaction. Being members of a religious group, the expectations from script (social norm), from others (others in the interaction situation), and from audience (reference groups) are important factors that may influence the behaviour of religious believers in social interaction. It means that religious doctrine, religious peers, and religious groups may influence the religious believers' behaviour. It is important to recognize that different religion may have different doctrine and different individual may have different religious group membership. But, as it is said already, the similarities can finally be found. The similarities assumed in this dissertation are, in all religions, there are beliefs in immortals (ancestors or God), the presence of immortals in the beyond.

1.2 The Different Characteristics Between the Religious Believers and Others

Because it is assumed first that religious believers may have something in common in social interaction, it is assumed second that the people who have religious beliefs may have something different from the people who do not have religious beliefs in social interaction. Then it is possible to distinguish the believers from the non-believers. Structural role theory helps researchers to develop an "ideal type" (a methodological tool by Max Weber) in social interaction analysis. Although the facts in reality may not be exactly the same as the ideal type, by comparing the facts in reality with the ideal type, the acquirement of the knowledge of the facts becomes easy. According to this thinking, social interaction in this research can be divided into the interaction with the beliefs in the presence of immortals and the interaction with the beliefs in the absence of immortals. To suppose that interaction happens in the situation of immortals (ancestors or God) being present or absent, how do people interact with each other and with immortals? Are there any differences between the two situations?

1.3 The Possibilities Contradicting With the First Two Assumptions

It is also assumed that there are possibilities that the facts in reality may contradict the first two assumptions. It means that the common characteristics of the religious believers in social interaction are not obvious, further more, the different characteristics between the religious believers and others are not obvious. Not everyone who has religious beliefs behaves in exactly the same way because the role expectations connected with a religious group or organization are not fully detailed and because religious believers who belong to a religious group or organization may have their own orientations toward the role. Society is a big "furnace". Everyone is "smelted" in it. Unless a person lives in a fictitious land of peace, he or she may be influenced by all kinds of factors. What they assume about others' action and what they inform others about themselves may not simply conform to role expectations. They may modify their roles. If it is so, another kind structure which is different from the structures in the first two assumptions will be found in social interaction.

2. Religious Beliefs

All religions have a suit of concepts which explain their beliefs, form a suit of conceptual systems, and construct a certain religious outlook. The main religious concepts are the concept of spirit and the concept of God. According to the categories of the concepts, religious beliefs can be divided into the same aspects as well (Lu Daji 1998: p.104). Beliefs are something accepted as true or real, according to the definition in dictionary. Religious beliefs, tend to revolve around five basic areas: humans found themselves in a predicament; humans need a way to resolve the predicament; there exists something transcendent that assists humans or is the goal of humans' existence; this something can be known or approached in some specified way; humans must do something to achieve salvation or liberation (Peterson, Hasker, Reichenbach and Basinger 1998: pp.8-10).

2.1 The Beliefs in the Spirit

The beliefs in the spirit refer to a supernatural existence which is inside the individuals, gives life to the individuals, and dominates all activities of the individuals. The characteristics of the spirit are: it is the dominator of all behaviour of the individuals; it may leave the individual's body and move about independently; it will not die along with the dying of the individual's body (Lu Daji 1998: pp.105-124). The immortal spirit is called soul.

Because of the belief in the concept of the soul, people imagine the life after death. On the one hand, they arrange a place for the soul of the dead; on the other hand, they draw a picture of the life of the dead: to continue the life in this world and to deserve the retribution in next world. People believe that the whole process of their life associates with the spirit and is the result of the domination and manipulation of the spirit. So they try to contact it either by praying to it in order to get help from it or by manipulating it in order to make use of it (Lu Daji 1998: pp.124-141). Harold Coward in "Life after Death in World Religion" answers the questions: Is there a life after death? What is it like? It offers reference to the readers to examine the differences and similarities in the way that different religions respond to the questions (Coward 1997: p.1). According to the book, the following examples illustrate how people in different religions view their life associating with the spirit, namely death and life after death.

Classical Judaism (comparing with Modern Judaism from ca. 1750) saw death as the end of a meaningful form of life or the end of a meaningful relationship to God. The dead did not become wholly extinct, but entered the underworld. Each person will be judged and his or her spirit will join those who are saved and destined for happiness or those who are condemned and destined for the underworld. The righteous will go to paradise while the wicked will go to hell. What sort of body will those have who are raised from the dead? The spiritual body, in Greek the *soma*. It is an incorrupted body, the body of a person who has been redeemed from corruption. The corrupted physical body, in Greek the *sarx,* cannot inherit the Kingdom. Judaism's approach to life after death is the foundation for Christianity and Islam as well, according to Coward (Coward 1997: pp.11-27).

Christianity views that Jesus' sacrificial death was a means of salvation for all people. Everyone of us is in a state of corruption, which has come from the fact that our ancestors disobeyed God. We all inherit their rebellious state. The inherited moral corruption is the source of our physical corruption, that is death. We are able to recognize that we are sinful and we may want to reform ourselves and turn back to God. But we do not have the inner power to make this change. The role of Christ is to reconcile us to God and give us this power.

His death was not a consequence of sin. It was wholly unmerited. In raising him from the dead, God has said that those who repent and accept Christ will be forgiven and resurrected. This will not spare them from dying but it will give them the reassurance that they will be raised as Christ was and be spared from corruption (Coward 1997: pp.31-46).

Islam views that death is a passageway from earthly life to the hereafter. God Allah alone is the sovereign of both realms. The life in this world is short. Only the life in the hereafter is the home to return. There is a belief that everyone will be judged in the tomb soon after death. The deceased will be visited by two angels, who make the dead person sit up in the grave in order to answer questions regarding faith, the uniqueness of God and the identity of Mahammed. If the dead answers correctly, he or she is left alone until the resurrection and the day of judgement. If the dead answers incorrectly, he or she will be recompensed with a punishment, deserve the burning. There is a day of resurrection. Paradise is the reward for those who abide by God's law and hell is the penalty for those who rebel against it. Only God knows the hour of resurrection. For Muslims, the hour is signalled by terrifying portents (Coward 1997: pp.48-62).

Buddhism does not agree that God created the world and that the spirit is immortal. If one agrees that God created the world, it means that everything in the world is arranged by God, therefore it will lose the meaning of man's effort. If one agrees that the spirit is immortal, it means that his spirit is immortal, he will indulge in the spirit of himself. Buddhism adopted the general Indian views of assuming that life is a changing but endless process, whereas death is only one of its recurring phases. The energy that keeps this process going is karma, it means action. In classical India this endless chain of lives was perceived as suffering. From Buddhist point of view, death is a transformation which provides opportunity to move the process forward toward enlightenment. One cannot be reborn but rather continues as the result of what he has done in his life or lives. The moment of death is an awareness of not only a turning point of recurring phase but also an opportunity to look beyond the ordinary existence (Coward 1997: pp.87-90). So it is not an immortal spirit but the mind of human beings that has the ability of continuity. The body dies, words and deeds will continue forming a new life and enduring the mutual promotion of cause and effect. Words and deeds will be the subject of samsara (Mu Zhongjian 2000: p.296).

Taoism is a religion which pays attention to the life in this world. For Taoism life is happiness and death is unhappiness. To cultivate oneself according to the Taoist doctrine on the basis of this life in order to attain the highest realm of life, be reborn (cast off one's old self) and live forever, is the goal. Taoism does not agree with the view that God determines man's life and death. Instead it focuses on keeping in good health and cultivating one's moral characters (Mu Zhongjian 2000: p.259).

2.2 The Beliefs in God

The belief in god is a reflection of the interpersonal relationship to religion. That is the relationship between humans and God. Humans are the believers and worshipers while God is believed and worshiped. Humans are the subjects of the belief and worship while God is the object of the belief and worship. The important point is not whether there is a god in a certain religion but how to understand the God in different religions and what kind of nature humans give to God. What is God? God is the existence of the supernatural. God is regarded as something humanized; God is regarded as something sacred (Lu Daji 1998: pp.151-155).

There are two ways of making something sacred by humans: one is to attach human nature to an object which has no human nature originally and to make it become a humanized God; the other is to abstract human nature from humans and to make it become an independent substance. Both ways are that of the objectified human nature. The foundation of sacred human nature is social relations. The nature of social relations determines the nature of humans, and the nature of humans determines the nature of God. The changes in the social relations determine the changes of the human nature and determine the changes of the nature of God (Lu Daji 1998: pp.155-158).

To believe in God means to believe in God's will and God's miracle. God has wills and can manipulate the natural world and human beings. God has morals and often concerns the natural world and societal affairs by supporting or opposing nature and humans. God has wisdom and may show his wisdom and express his willingness to others. God has power and can use this power to realize his intentions. It is only God who has this power which is supreme. God can make miracles according to his wills, the miracles are special and abnormal. The miracles in religion are different from the miracles in the natural word. Only those which cannot be explained by the natural laws can be defined as religious miracles (Lu Daji 1998: pp.206-258).

2.3 The Similarities of the Beliefs

From the brief description of the spirit and God, we can assume that people experience different lives in this world and therefore, may have different imagination of the life in the next world (according to the beliefs of the spirit). People have different social relations in society and may therefore have different relations with God (according to the beliefs in God). In spite of the many differences, there are similarities: all believe that there is a world beyond, and that people will live in that world after they leave this world. The concept relating to this is immortal. In some religions, the immortals are regarded as something humanized, such as God. In some religions, the immortals are regarded as something sacred, such as ancestors. In fact, the nature of all immortals in all religions is the nature of humans. The humanized immortals are the sacred humans. People can constantly communicate with them and have a permanent relationship with them. And they themselves will go there, to continue the life in this world and to be rewarded or punished in the next world. Though there are differences among different religions, people with different religions may answer the same question, for example, the view about the dead in the beyond, differently, the similarities can be found finally. In my research, the focus will be on the belief in immortals, to be more exact, the presence of the immortals in the beyond.

2.4 What is Religion?

People are influenced by what they constantly see and hear about religion but their definitions of religion are vary widely. They may concentrate on the objects of the religious beliefs (such as God) to define religion. It means that religion is a belief in and worship of the supernatural. They may concentrate on the subjects of the religious beliefs (such as individual) to define religion. It means that religion is a mysterious experience of human-supernatural communication. They may concentrate on the environment of the religious beliefs (such as society) to define religion. It means that religion is a way of fulfilling the social needs (Lu Daji 1998: pp.51-64).

Alan Aldridge in "Religion in the Contemporary World" classifies two types of definitions of religion: broader inclusive definitions and narrower exclusive definitions. Inclusive definitions of religion are functional, to define religion by what it does, for example, "Religion is a way of fulfilling social needs". Exclusive definitions of religion are substantive, to define religion by what it is, for example, "Religion is a belief and worship to the supernatural" (Aldridge 2000: pp.26-30).

Scholars of religious studies found that religion as a social phenomenon has some basic elements or dimensions. These elements or dimensions can be categorized into two kinds: one is the internal ones of religion, the religious beliefs or thoughts and religious experiences or emotions; the other is the external ones of religion, the religious behaviours or activities and religious organizations or systems. The relations of the elements or dimensions are: religious belief is the core of religion; religious experience is the psychological reflection of the belief; religious behaviour is the presentation of the belief and the experience; religious organization is the result of the systemized religious life (Lu Daji 1998: pp.74-77). On the basis of this opinion, religion can be regarded as a social consciousness concerning supernatural forces, a behaviour of believing in and worshiping of the forces, or a cultural system of the normalized consciousness and behaviours (Lu Daji 1998: 78-87). Or in another words, religion is assumed as something constituted by a set of beliefs, actions, and experiences, both personal and corporate, organized around a concept of an Ultimate Reality (Peterson, Hasker, Reichenbach and Basinger 1998: pp.8-10).

There are many definitions of religion. Each of the definitions may emphasize certain aspects of religion and neglect others. For example, if religion is defined as a belief and worship to the supernatural, it fails to incorporate the idea that supernatural forces have some influence or control upon the world, a notion that always accompanies belief in the supernatural (Haralambos and Holborn 1990: p.645). Ronald Johnstone in "Religion in Society: A Sociology of Religion" introduced J. M. Yinger's useful imagery in speaking to this issue (Johnstone

1997: pp.2-3): "He frames the objection to the empirical study of religion with the question: how is it possible to see a stained-glass window from outside? That is the beauty and the message or picture of church's stained glass window is visible only when one is inside and can see the sunlight shining through. However, the view from the inside constitutes only part of what can be learned about the window. Only from outside, for example, can the viewer appreciate the exterior framework or context within which that window exists. Furthermore, pieces of information potentially important to understanding the significance of the window that has nothing to do with viewing it from inside or outside for that matter who built it, who installed it. We can also consider the reason it was installed." We view religion not only from the inside as a believer but also from the outside as an observer, then from beyond as a researcher. In order to illustrate Yinger's imagery, a picture can be made (See Figure 1).

Figure 1: To See a Stained-Glass Window

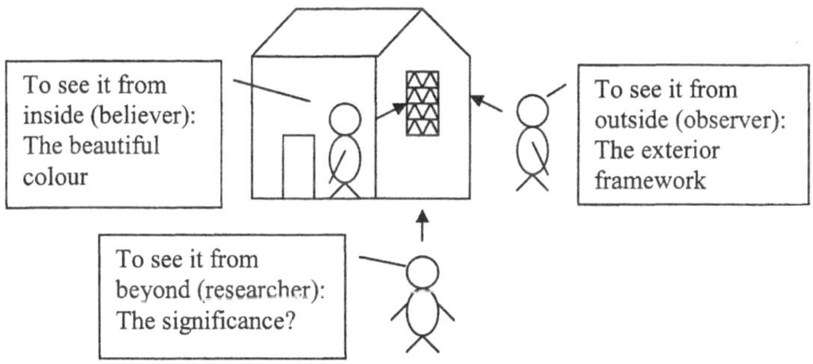

One of the important questions is needed to raise here: who makes the definition, for example, religion is defined by a believer or by a researcher? Many believers call themselves religious but some of their beliefs may not be regarded as religious from the view of a researcher. Each of the researchers has his or her definition of religion but it may not be agreed by others. The argument is not the focus here. Instead the focus is, in research, religious believers are identified by researchers while researchers define religion according to their approaches. Classical approaches to religion in sociology are good examples of this. It helps us to see how sociologists defined religion.

To see religion as the product of the human tendency to seek to understand the world and of human reasoning from their observation and experience is called intellectualist approach. One of the representative intellectualist thinkers is **August Comte**. His evolutionary scheme of the development of human thought, which he thought is the key to the development of society, was set out in his book "The Positive Philosophy". He thought that in the intellectual development of humanity there are three distinct stages, namely theological, metaphysical and positive. Comte did not think that with the arrival of science, religion would disappear entirely. Religion, he thought, is not only an attempt to explain and understand reality but also the unifying principle of human society. Since the science which is concerned with understanding the principles of social unity and cohesion is sociology, then the new religion would be a kind of applied sociology (Hamilton 1995: pp.21-27).

To see religion as a compensating and comforting illusion which would eventually be dispensed with as human beings lost their need for illusions is another kind of approach to sociology and also to psychology. One of the important thinkers in sociology is **Karl Marx.** Religion for Marx is essentially the product of a class society. His ideas on religion are part of his general theory of alienation in class societies. Religion is seen as both a product of alienation and expression of class interests. It is a tool for the oppression of the subordinate class in society, and expression of protest against oppression, a form of consolation in the face of oppression. There is no systematic treatment of religion in Marx's writings. What he had to say consists of many scattered passages throughout his works. The most extensive passage occurs in his "Contribution to the Critique of Hegel's Philosophy of Right" which contains his overall approach to the analysis of religion. According to Marx, man makes religion, religion does not make man. Religious distress is the expression of real distress and the protest against real distress. It is the opium of the people. The abolition of religion as the illusory happiness of the people is required for real happiness (Hamilton 1995: pp.80-86).

To see religion in the context of the existing society and its role in society as the main focus is a functionalist approach on religion. This kind of approach is influenced by **Emile Durkheim**, his famous book "The Elementary Forms of the Religious Life". Religion, for Durkheim is the collective force of society over the individual. Religion is a system of ideas with which the individuals represent to themselves the society of which they are members and the obscure but intimate relations which they have with it. Religion is also a system of action, involves rituals. Rituals, for Durhkeim are essential maintaining group cohesion and are believed by participants to bring about some desirable state of affairs or prevent an undesirable one. His concept of religion as social cement is different from the Marxist metaphor of religion as a social opium (Halmilton 1995: pp.97-108).

To see religion as a provider of meaning in the face of what threatens to be a meaningless world is one kind of approach in sociology. The essence of religion is that it is a response to the threat of meaninglessness in human life, and it is an attempt to see the world as a meaningfully reality. Among the earlier theorists, **Max Weber** laid the ground work for such an approach and for the synthesis of the various strands from which the religious life is woven. The most explicit discussion of this is in his work "The Economic Ethic of the World Religions". Whatever fortune befalls a person, whether it is good or bad, it cannot be accepted as mere chance. It must be explained and justified in some way. Religion is fundamentally a response to the difficulties and injustice of life which attempts to make sense of them and enables people to cope with them and feel more confident when faced by them (Hamilton 1995: pp.137-146).

To see religion is one form of social life, under which there are many contents, is another kind of approach in sociology. The representative scholar of the approach is **Georg Simmel**. In his book "Sociology, the Study on the Forms of Social Interaction" Simmel pointed out that the interaction in the social reality contains a similar model. It is so called the form of interaction. The human interaction is very complicated. If we cannot find some common forms from the complicated phenomena, the study cannot be deepened. Many human relationships harbour a religious element. The relationships have a variety of content, but share a similar form. This form has a common tone that can be described only as religion. All religiosity contains peculiar quality. This quality is contained in many other relationships, and gives them a tone that distinguishes them from relationships based on non-religious qualities (Helle and Nieder 1997: pp.101-120).

If we agree with Simmel that religion is one form of social life, we should study the form of interaction: interaction in the form of person to person and in the form of person to supernatural beings. Actually we study how the person-immortal interaction influences the person-person interaction. If we agree with Weber that religion is a provider of meanings, we should study how religion interprets social phenomena. We do study or compare how people interpret social phenomena in the process of interaction (the subjective interpretation). If we agree with Durhkeim that religion plays a role or function in society, we should study the influence of religion on interaction. We do study the influence of religious beliefs on interaction (the objective function). If we agree with Marx that religion is a compensating and comforting illusion, we should study how religion fulfills the needs of any sides of the interaction. It stresses more of the individual rather than both sides of the interaction. If we agree with Comte that religion is a product of human development, we should study the evolution of religion. It is true that along with the development of society, religion itself has undergone changes, but this is not the main focus of the research.

Previous research indicates that religious studies involve both how to define religion (what religion is) and how to approach religion (what religion does). In my research, the definition of religion is not discussed at the beginning temporarily. How do we distinguish people who are religious and who are non-religious? By whether or not they believe in immortals in the beyond.

3. Social Interaction

Social interaction means that people, in order to fulfil certain needs, act on each other. It is the activity of people acting toward each other. A single person's action cannot be called an interaction. It is a meaningful activity. The actors know not only the motivation behind the interaction but also the possible result of the interaction (Han Mingmo 1993: pp.52-53).When interaction occurs between two sides, two things happen almost simultaneously. Each side in an interaction situation is sending words and cues and receiving and processing words and cues as they come in from the other side. The important feature of interaction is the way that people use their minds to interpret the words and cues of another, deduce their meaning, and respond accordingly (Kammeger, Ritzer and Yetman 1997: pp.91-92).

One the one hand, interaction goes on within the context of the cultural values and the social norms. Once the values and the norms are internalized by the individuals during the process of socialization, interaction is regarded as patterned. The individuals need not think it over when they interact with others. They keep themselves within the bounds of values and norms. Everybody has a status which is a socially recognized position in a social system and a role which is the behaviour generally expected of one who occupies a particular status. On the other hand, however, not everyone in a particular status behaves in exactly the same way. Because the role expectations connected with a status are not fully detailed. Role expectations are not so precisely stated or understood that every detail of expected behaviour is clear. Because individuals who hold statuses may have their own orientations toward the role, interaction is regarded as varied. The individuals need to use their brains when they interact with others. They do not simply conform to role expectations, they also actively modify their roles (Kammeger, Ritzer, and Yetman 1997: pp.93-95). Jonathan H. Turner in "The Structure of Sociological Theory" introduces two theories: structural role theory and process role theory. The patterned interaction is described as a play and the non-patterned interaction as a game.

How to understand the two theories? Does it mean that any social interaction can be regarded as either a play or a game? Or does it mean that any social interaction can be regarded as both a play and a game? The following content is a brief introduction to Turner's theories and the theories concerned in order to have a theoretical basis for the empirical analysis.

3.1 Structural Role Theory

To use a metaphor to describe the players on the stage and the actors in society, Turner writes: "Just as players have a defined part to play, so actors in society occupy positions. Just as players must follow a written script, so actors in society must follow norms. Just as players must obey the orders of a director, so actors in society must conform to the dictates of those with power. Just as players must react to each other's performance on the stage, so members of society must adjust their responses to one another. Just as players respond to audience, so actors in society take the role of various audiences. Just as players with varying abilities and capacities bring to each role their unique interpretations, so actors with varying self-concepts and role-playing skills have their own styles of interaction." If interaction is regarded as a play, the images of society and the individual can be assumed as: in the concept of stage are assumptions about the nature of social organization; in the concept of players are assumptions about the nature of the individual; in the vision of men and women as merely players, are assumptions about the relationship of individuals and social organizations (Turner 1991: pp.410-424).

Social organization is composed of various networks of statuses and expectations. Status networks are classified into forms ranging from small groups to large organizations. Expectations are categorized into three types: expectations from the script (social norms), expectations from other players (others in an interaction situation), and expectations from the audience (reference groups). Usually status networks are rarely analysed independently of the types of expectations because the types of expectations that typify particular networks of positions represent the networks characters.

Individuals are generally conceptualized in two basic attributes: self-related characteristics and role-playing skills. The self-related concepts are diverse but concerned with the impact of them on individuals' interpretation of the expectations in a particular status. Role-playing skills denote those capacities of individuals to perceive various types of expectations with their competence and role-playing styles. These two attributes are also interrelated because self conceptions will mediate the perception of expectations and the way roles are enacted.

The relationship between individuals and society is that the individuals who are incumbent in statuses and who employ self conceptions and role-playing skills adjust various types of expectations. There are three components of roles receiving varying degrees of emphasis which makes the articulation between individuals and society differ. When conceptual emphasis is placed upon the expectations on individuals in status positions (prescribed roles), the social world is assumed to be composed of prescriptions, the individuals' behaviour conforms to the expectation of a particular status. When conceptual emphasis falls upon the perceptions and interpretations of expectations (subjective roles), the social world is seen as structured individuals' subjective assessments of the interaction situation, the individuals' interpretation and adjustment of the expectations becomes primary. When conceptual emphasis is given to overt behaviour (enacted roles), the social world is viewed as a network of interrelated behaviours, the individual's role enactment is stressed.

The general causal sequence among these analytical units is that specific expectations of social organization influence the individuals, their self-related process, role-playing skills and enacted role behaviour. As to the interrelations among expectations, self conceptions, role-playing skills and overt behaviour, different types of expectations influence self conceptions, role-playing skills and overt behaviour. While, certain feedbacks should also be emphasized. The emphasis is on the degree of embeddedness of self in certain groups, the degree of intimacy with specific others, and degree of internalization of certain norms. The emphasis is also on the impact of overt behaviour on the expectations of others. With the reference of Turner's original figure (Turner 1991: p.417), the structural interaction can be mapped as following (See Figure 2).

Figure 2: The Structured Interaction

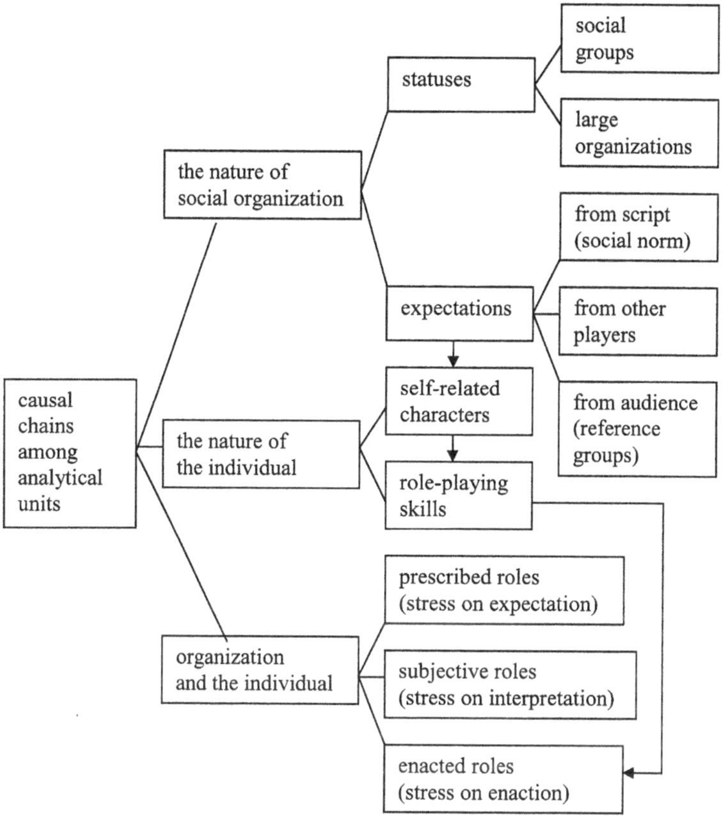

3.2 Process Role Theory

To counter structure role-theory, sociologists raised a series of questions: Does the structural conception of role add anything that is not covered by the concept of normative expectation? Can the structural analysis of roles deal with roles that are not lodged in some organizational structure? Can structural orientations to roles deal with situations where new roles are created or old ones changed? A series of unsolved issues are handled by sociologists in their studies: Whether or not roles are acts of conformity to norms or creative constructions of actors? Whether or not roles are inventories of specific behaviours or more general gestalts and configurations of meaning about lines of conduct? Whether or not roles are fixed and predetermined or do individuals negotiate which roles they are going to play in a situation? To answer these questions, there is an alternative theory: process role theory (Turner 1991: pp.425-446).

The process of interaction is not only role taking but also role making. Instead of putting themselves in the positions of others in order to evaluate how others see them and their behaviour (role-taking), people assume others are playing a role and thus make an effort to discover the underlying role behind others' acts. They seek to make a role for themselves in all social situations by emitting cues to others that give them claim on a particular role (role-making). They behave more actively than passively. For example: In order to ask for a help from others, you explain your difficulties to others who you assumed can do you a favour.

As people interact with one another, they assess behaviour not in terms of its conformity to imputed norms or positions in a social structure but in regard to its consistency. People seek to group one another's behaviour into coherent wholes or gestalts, by doing so, they can make sense of one another's actions, anticipate one another's behaviour, and adjust to one another's responses. For example: If somebody made a promise, you may ask, does it conform to or contradict with his normal behaviour? Conform, trust it. Contradict, doubt ......?

Interaction is always a tentative process, a process of continuously testing the conception one has of the role of the other. People are constantly interpreting additional cues emitted by others and seeing if these new cues are consistent with the previous ones. A particular role to another person will persist only as long as it provides a stable framework for interaction. For example: If somebody made a mistake, you may ask, does he make this mistake regularly or occasionally? Regularly, criticize him. Occasionally, forgive him.

People seek to verify the behaviours and cues of others', then they make their own roles. The efforts at verification are achieved by the application of external and internal criteria. The internal criteria are the degree to which an actor perceives a role to facilitate interaction. The external criteria involve assessment of a role by important others, relevant groups, or common standards. For example: If you want to select a supervisor, you may ask, is he worthy of the name? Yes, OK. No, look for another.

Humans develop attitudes and feelings out of their interacting with others. They attempt to present themselves in ways that will reinforce their self-conceptions. Since others will always seek to determine an actor's role, it becomes necessary for an actor to inform others through behaviours about the degree to which self is anchored in a role. Thus actors will signal one another about their self-identity and the extent to which their role is consistent with their self-conception, for example, roles not consistent with a person's self-conception will likely be played with considerable distance and disdain. For example: If you are happy to be a member of a church, you may go there often. The following figure illustrates the process role theory according to the understanding of Turner's theory (See Figure 3).

3.3 Basic Principles of the Theories

According to Jonathan Turner, social interaction can be viewed from two aspects. On the one hand, it is viewed as structured. It produces patterned behaviour. On the other hand, it is viewed as varied. In the process of the interaction, statuses and roles may be modified and changed over time. Trying to understand Turner's theories is that any social interaction cannot not be simply classified as a play or a game. It should be viewed from two aspects. If we view the interaction from an inductive way from specific cases to a general character, it is patterned. If we view the interaction from a deductive way from a general structure to specific cases, it is varied but under a general structure. It is not an issue if human interaction "is" structured or varied but an issue if human interaction is "viewed" as structured or varied. People often say: "It should be that way normally but it just depends". It should be that way according to the rules but it just depends on the person and the situation. It reveals that people are having a game in a play.

Figure 3: Process of Role Making

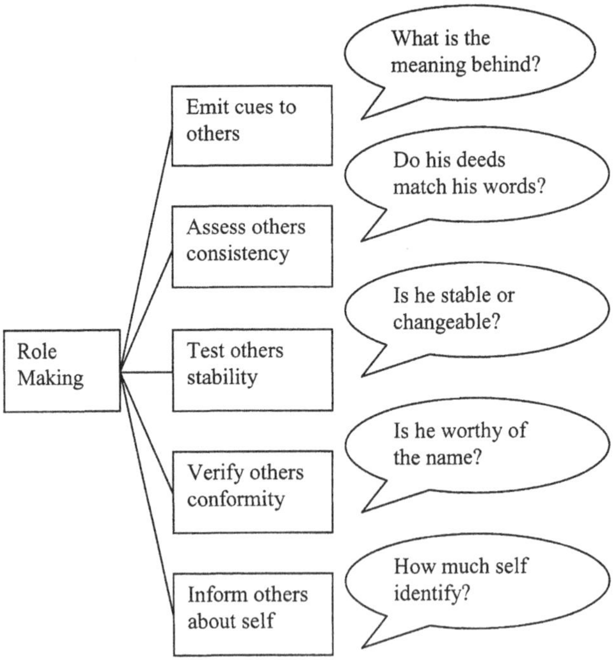

To summarize the two perspectives, social interaction has the following basic principles: (1) Society is a stage like the stage for a play. Individuals are players like those who enact on the stage. (2) The stage can be regarded as a network of variously interrelated statuses, in accord with the statuses, there are a suit of expectations. (3) The players who occupy a particular status enact on the stage according to the relevant expectations. (4) Because of the culture differences, the stages in different societies (different cultural values and different social norms) may be different. (5) Because of the individual differences, the players with different self-related characters and role-playing skills may enact differently. (6) Social interaction, in a general framework, is viewed as patterned; in a specific situation, is viewed as varied.

3.4 Types of Social Interaction

It is said briefly in the introduction that social interaction can be categorized into many kinds. Different criteria have different categories. Among the different categories, I concentrate in this study on the interaction between individuals by the way of face to face contact. In everyday life, everybody has many opportunities to interact with a variety of persons and in a variety of settings: to interact with the relatives in the family, to interact with the neighbours in the community, to interact with the colleagues in the working unit, to interact with the pedestrians in the street......or to interact with ancestors or god in the beyond. Some people are together from morning to night, they closely associate, for example, intimates; Some people just brush past, they keep their distance, for example, strangers. What about those who live in different world, here and the beyond? Considering the interaction and the relationship between the humans and ancestors or god, social interaction can be categorized into one with the presence of the immortals in the beyond and the other with the absence of the immortals in the beyond.

To Interact with the Strangers

There are many definitions of the stranger. Georg Simmel, for example, defines minorities in society under the concept of stranger. A stranger, may come from a faraway country, and he is now close at hand. A stranger is a person from afar who is now close at hand because he has come to stay, although he might leave again. The stranger's distinctive position is to be close or distant to a group at the same time. The integration of closeness and distance within the interpersonal relationship means that something close is distant, whereas being confronted with something alien means that something distant has come close (Helle 2001: pp.161-168).

Besides of the stranger which Simmel defines, there is another kind in everyday life. That is the person who may not come from a faraway country (or may come from a faraway country possibly), but we have never met him before and known nothing about him. To differentiate between the two kinds of strangers, two terms can be used: cultural stranger and biographical stranger. The term of cultural stranger refers to those who have no shared frameworks for interpreting social reality and occupy different symbolic worlds. The term of biographical stranger refers to those who have never met before and have no knowledge of one another's life histories (Karp 1986: pp.97-99). Sometimes two people feel like old friends at the first meeting. Sometimes two people know each other for a long time but never get along well.

When strangers confront one another, they usually feel uncertain about each other. Usually social norms require people to trust others, assuming that others are harmless. But there is always some doubt about the true motives, goals of others. So the paradox that people must trust and doubt others at the same time always exists in social interaction. It is true that ordered interaction proceeds on the general assumption of trust, but people can never be certain that such an assumption is perfectly safe. How do people make a judgment about strangers? It depends on immediate observations of the strangers, the strangers' social and physical attributes and the observers' interpretations. Social attributes include a person's age, gender, race, education, occupation, and class. Physical attributes include a person's height, weight, looking, posture, discourse, and grooming. Interpretations rely on commonly accepted stereotypes in a certain culture and interpreter's personal characteristics (Karp 1986: pp.99-120).

Strangers typically confront each other in anonymous situations. The structure of public behaviours between strangers is reinforced by efforts to maintain the norm of anonymity. The norm is shared and known about by all participants, is designed to limit the accessibility of unacquainted individuals to one another. People make efforts to remain anonymous and to maintain their privacy. In the effort to maintain anonymity and keep privacy, strangers in public places adopt elaborate strategies to avoid one another. This does not mean that they are entirely uninvolved with one another. Strangers in public places also adopt mechanisms to produce ordered relationships. Social activities demand some degree of cooperation. A balance between noninvolvement and cooperation requires to minimize involvement and maximize order (Karp 1986: pp.99-120). To express the interaction between strangers according to the above contents, a figure can be made as following (See Figure 4).

Though strangers normally remain anonymous and reduce involvement in one another, they may not be always the same. Sometimes there are situations in which people can begin to dissolve the strangeness between them. The concept of uncertainty with strangers can be reduced in certain circumstances. Strangers can become intimates (Karp 1986: pp.99-120). What are intimates? Friends, lovers, relatives...... They are intimates because they are close and they know each other well. To be close with others and make friends with others is a human need. Humans need intimacy.

Figure 4: Interaction Between Strangers

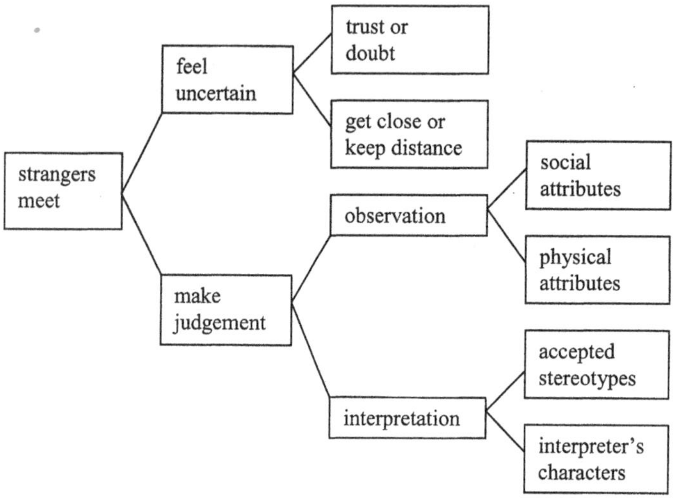

To Interact with the Intimates

How to define intimacy? It depends on the general values of the society in which individuals live and the specific values of the groups to which they belong or with which they identify (Karp 1986: pp.130-139). Intimacy can be divided into two basic concepts: intimate interactions and intimate relationships. Intimate interactions are dialogues between people and do not require the presence of a relationship to occur. Intimate relationships imply a series of interaction between two individuals knowing each other (Prager 1995: pp.18-20). Sometimes a man and a woman "fall in love" at first sight; Sometimes a man and a woman lived together for a long time but separated in the end.

Intimate interactions have two components: intimate behaviour which refers to the actual observable behaviour people engage in when interacting intimately and intimate experiences which are the feelings and perceptions people have because of their intimate interactions. Intimate behaviour is shared and personal. Intimates may share personal thoughts, emotional expressions, and body language. They may also share each other's interests, feelings, and try to understand each other. Partners share what they do and they would not do so under impersonal circumstances (Prager 1995: pp.20-23).

Intimate relationships are those in which the partners share regular intimate interactions, feel affection for one another, trust one another, and have cohesion. Affection, trust, and cohesion seem to be necessary conditions for sustaining intimacy in a relationship. Most intimate relationships may have many other characteristics that are important to sustaining intimacy. Relationships lacking affection, trust, or cohesion seem unlikely, to sustain intimate interaction (Prager 1995: pp.23-25). Prager on intimate interaction and intimate relationship can be mapped as following (See Figure 5).

According to Karen Prager, intimate interaction happens under certain circumstances. There are four levels of contextual factors which influence intimate behaviour. The first level is the interaction situation. It refers to the nature of the occasion and the physical surroundings. The second level is the personal relationship. It includes the individual histories and characteristics of each participant, the history and definition of their relationship, and outcomes of those histories. Because of their individual histories and inherited proclivities, people may develop certain characteristic ways of thinking and behaving that affect their intimate interactions. The third level is the reference group. It refers to the social groups and networks to which the individual belongs to. Groups, both small and large, seem likely to affect intimate interaction via group norms.

The forth level is the sociocultural system. Sociocultural factors usually manifest themselves as norms. Sociocultural norms are difficult to assess because they are often implicit and are therefore outside awareness. Exposure to alternatives is often the only means by which sociocultural norms become evident to people. When the norms become explicit, people do observe them, and they react negatively to others who do not (Prager 1995: pp.171-178).

Figure 5: The Components of Intimacy

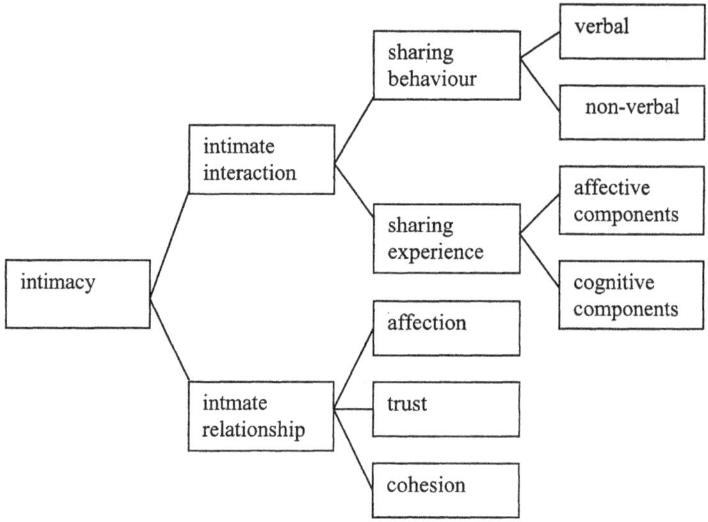

4. Religious Beliefs and Social Interaction

Before we talk about religious beliefs and social interaction, it is necessary to talk briefly about attitude and behaviour. Attitude is a concept which is often used in social psychology. Attitude is an individual's stable psychological tendency to a certain thing, concept or other people. Attitude consists of cognitive element, emotional element, and behaviour tendency. Cognitive element refers to an individual's psychological impression on the objects outside. It includes facts, knowledge, beliefs, and so on. Cognitive element is the basis of attitude. Emotional element refers to an individual's positive or negative evaluation to a certain matter and mood or feelings derived from the evaluation. Emotion is the core of attitude. Behaviour tendency refers to an individual's prepared response or behaviour to other people or other things outside. It may influence an individual's action toward the people or other things outside (Shen Decan 1995: pp.112-116).

The three elements of attitude depend on each other and coordinate each other. The cognition about other people or other things influences the individual's evaluation, proceeding to their intended behaviour. Attitude has the characteristic of being ready to do something. It will influence the behaviour which is adopted towards the objects. People's attitude and behaviour are often closely connected. People's attitude in many circumstances determines people's behaviour. For example: one person would communicate with another if the one likes the other. But attitude does not completely correspond to behaviour. For example: one person says from his lips that he likes another but actually is tired of the other in heart (Shen Decan 1995: pp.112-116, pp.149-156). If sociology helps us to understand how influential factors affect the individuals from outside, social psychology helps us to understand how influential factors affect the individual inside.

4.1 The Relationship of Religious Beliefs and Social Interaction

The concept of attitude and behaviour relates to the relationship between belief and interaction. Belief is one of the important influential elements of attitude, it is one of the cognitive components of attitude. If the cognition about other people or other things influences the individual's evaluation, proceeding to their intended behaviour, the intended behaviour will become an observed behaviour. If the observed behaviour is that of people acting toward each other, symbolically communicating to each other, social interaction occur. The following example may illustrate how attitudes (beliefs) influence behaviour (interaction):

A person believes that Chinese Qigong can make the humans be healthy and can cure the sickness (cognitive element). Hence he may have a mysterious and dependent feeling to Qigong (emotional element). If asking him to make a selection of a physical exercise, he may select to practise Qigong (behaviour tendency). If a friend says to him that he feels unwell, he may say to his friend: come, let me treat you by Qigong (interaction). If the friend believes in Qigong as well, he will interpret the treatment as a therapy (interpretation) and accept it (feedback). Then he may say: I feel better (experience). If the friend does not believe in Qigong, he may interpret the treatment as a mischief and refuse it. If the friend refuses it, the interaction of the two will be cornered in a difficult situation (See Figure 6).

The example reveals the role of beliefs in the process of interaction. There is a Chinese saying: It is efficacious if you believe it. The "efficacious" is produced by the beliefs. It is mentioned in the introduction that people interact not only with others but with themselves. There are two kinds of behaviours: one is the overt one which is the actual performance by actors; the other is the covert one which is the thinking process involving symbols and meanings. Beliefs just play a role when people interact with themselves. People with different beliefs may bestow things (words, artifacts, actions, etc.) with different meanings. Once the things are bestowed with meanings, they are no longer simple things, they are symbols. People can symbolically communicate these meanings to other people.

"It allows people to transcend time, space, and even their own persons. They can imagine what it was like to live in the past or might be like to live in the future. They can transcend their own symbolically and imagine what the world is like from another person's point of view. It allows people to imagine a metaphysical reality, such as heaven or hell" (Ritzer 1992: p.351). People with religious beliefs may transcend time, space and themselves to imagine a metaphysical reality: to communicate or interact with the people in the beyond, the immortals.

Figure 6: The Role of Beliefs in Interaction

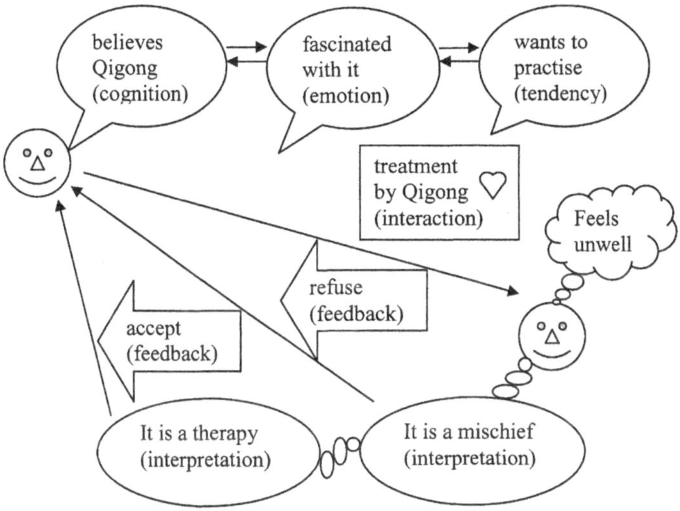

4.2 Experience the Interaction between Humans and Immortals

People with religious beliefs may have a special feeling to sacred things and may have psychological and spiritual experience towards sacred things. For example, some religious believers said that they sometimes communicate with

God directly and get inspiration from God directly. George Wall in "Religious Experience and Religious Beliefs" makes a judgement about religious and non-religious experience. If a person senses a unity with nature but senses nature as strictly physical, the experience is not religious, because it does not have a divinity. If a person has an experience of ecstasy while listening to music, the experience is not religious, because it does not have an awareness of divine presence. If a person senses that something unlucky will happen and it really happens, it is not a religious experience, because it does not have an awareness of divine presence. Wall defines that religious experience is direct awareness of or encounter with a divine being (Wall 1995: pp.10-11).

Michael Peterson and his colleagues in "Reason & Religious Belief" define that religious experience is an event that one lives through and of which one is conscious or aware. Religious experience is taken by the person to be some supernatural being or presence, a being related to God or some indescribable Ultimate Reality. Peterson and his colleagues introduce five types or possibilities: (1) Experience of God or Ultimate Reality mediated through a common, public, sensory object. For example, one might claim to see God in a sunset. Sunsets are not God but that in and through which God is encountered. (2) Experience of God or Ultimate Reality mediated through an unusual, public, sensory object. For example, one might claim to experience the supernatural through an appearance of a figure seen in a cloud. (3) Experience of God or Ultimate Reality mediated through private sensations that can be described in normal sensory language. For example, a person might claim to experience God in a dream. (4) Experience of God or Ultimate Reality mediated through private sensations that cannot be described in normal sensible language. For example, a person feels or claims to experience something but it cannot be spoken about. It is ineffable. (5) Experience of God or Ultimate Reality that is not mediated by any sensations. For example, a person claims to be intuitively and immediately aware of God or the one (Peterson, Hasker, Reichenbach and Basinger 1998: pp.19-22).

In reality, Peterson and his colleagues point out that perhaps few experiences fall neatly into one given type, for experiences contain richly diverse elements. It is more important to understand more generally the diversity of ways persons understanding their religious experiences, to understand what people really experience. Do they really experience God or Ultimate Reality or do they only interpret certain experiences religiously? Peterson and his colleagues introduced three different perspectives on the reality of religious experience suggested by philosophers: (1) Religious Experience as feeling: religious experience is a feeling of absolute or dependence upon a source or power that is distinct from the world. It is an affective rather than a cognitive experience. God can be grasped by reason. We can ascribe to god attributes but his holiness cannot be rationally known. We apprehend God's holiness by something that goes beyond the rational, by feeling. (2) Religious experience as perception: the religious experiencer is as the perceiver, God or Ultimate Reality is as the perceived object, the appearance or presence of God or Ultimate Reality to the experiencer is as the phenomenon. When we describe God's qualities, we describe how it would look under normal conditions, we use not phenomenal language but comparative concepts. (3) Religious experience as interpretation: embedded in the experiencer's understanding of their experience is a claim about its cause. Such persons believe that God exists. Their religious experience cannot be understood apart from their belief that they encountered God or Ultimate Reality. When people have an experience, they identify that experience under some set of concepts and beliefs. There is no uninterpreted datum that is experienced and then later interpreted. The experience itself is embedded both in some interpretation of the world and in some commitment to a certain set of religious beliefs and practices (Peterson, Hasker, Reichenbach and Basinger 1998: pp.22-29).

Kenneth Kammeyer and his colleagues in "Sociology, Experiencing Changing Societies" introduce that the religious experience can be categorized into four types in the order of the frequency with which each type of experience occurs. (1) Confirming religious experience: it is the most frequently reported one in their research. It is a feeling that the individual becomes aware of the existence or presence of the sacred. The sudden intensification of feeling may take a general form in which the individual experiences a sense of reverence, solemnity or calmness. Or the individual may have a awareness of the closeness of a divine being. (2) Responsive religious experience: it is marked by reciprocity rather than merely being made aware of the presence of the divine. The individual has a sense that the divine is responding to him or her as well. It involves an awareness of an external power controlling the individual. It can also produce a sense that the divine has chosen the individual. (3) Ecstatic religious experience: it involves not only confirming and responding to the divine but also a feeling of an intense and intimate emotional relationship with the sacred. For example, the individual senses that his or her soul or mind has left the body and is observing the body from outside. (4) Revelational religious experience: it is the least common type of religious experience. The individual receives confidential information from the sacred about the future (Kammeyer, Ritzer and Yetman 1997: pp.522-526).

4.3 Theoretical Examples of Human-Immortal Interaction

The studies of religious experience indicate that human-immortal interaction may occur in many circumstances. Some of the interactions can be described while some of the interactions can only be sensed (Peterson, Hasker, Reichenbach and Basinger, 1998). The human-immortal interaction might be something that people really experience or something that people interpret according to their beliefs (Peterson, Hasker, Reichenbach and Basinger, 1998). As to the religious believers, what do they experience in detail? Confirming, responding, or ecstatic to the immortals? All kinds (Kammeyer, Ritzer and Yetman, 1997). The following examples are only a few examples of human-immortal interaction which present theoretically how religious beliefs influence social interaction.

Self Concept by George H. Mead: The Immortals as Significant Others

George H. Mead in "Mind, Self, and Society" (Edited by Charles W. Morris, 1976) introduced the contents of his course "Social Psychology". His thoughts are regarded as some of the important components of the theory on social interaction. People's activities are not simply responses to the outside stimulus. The objective substance becomes a stimulating factor only when it is functioning. People adjust themselves according to the objective substance in the environment. The relationship between individual behaviours and objective environment also exists in social action. Mead synthesized several intellectual traditions and developed his own theory: mind, self and society. He accepted the behaviorism tradition and viewed that reinforcement guides and directs action. Combining with behaviorism and pragmatism he viewed that human beings seek to cope with their actual conditions and they learn those behavioral patterns which provide gratification. The gratification is the adjustment to social contexts. He also absorbed Darvinism and recognized that human beings are organisms seeking for a niche in which they can adapt. In the process of coping, adjusting, adapting and achieving the gratification to survive, human beings acquire mind and self as an adaptation to society (Turner 1991: pp.372-377).

In order to adjust to the social contexts and to adapt to society, the gestures which can provide gratification gained symbolic meanings. Both the sender and the receiver interpret them the same way, at last the interaction among people can be conducted by these gestures. With the development of social behaviour, symbols are developed as well and function in the process of action. Because the human mind has the capacity to use symbols to designate objects, to collect ways towards these objects, then to select a proper way to do, human beings developed the ability to understand symbols, to employ these symbols to take the role of other, and to imagine the way of role taking (Turner 1991: pp.372-377).

Because human beings can designate symbolically other actors, so they can symbolically represent themselves as an object in each interaction to assess it and to evaluate it. This is how the self concept is produced. One may see himself from the perspective of others and regard himself as an objective one. This self has an ability to select a proper way to communicate with specific others, to attribute the proper way to a general other. Then they have a self identity (Turner 1991: pp.372-377).

If the individuals interact with each other in an organized and patterned way depending upon the "mind", if the individuals evaluate themselves from the perspective of broad community depending upon the "self", a society is formed. Mead viewed society as a constructed phenomenon that arises out of the adjustive interactions among the individuals. At the same time, because the process of symbolic interaction is dynamic, society is changing as well. Both the static and the dynamic of society, occur through the processes of mind and self.

What may be the influence of the religious beliefs in social interaction according to Mead's theory? The significant others that people perceive may be different. Besides both sides of the interaction see themselves from the perspective of each other, the religious people may regard the perspectives of the immortals as an important reference.

Frame Analysis by Erving Goffman: The Immortals Playing a Role in Frame Forming

The early theory on interaction by Goffman is "Presentation of Self in Everyday Life". It analysed the way in which people portray their image when they interact with others. Then he moved away from his classic symbolic interactionist roots toward the study of the small-scale structures of social life. In "Frame Analysis", he tried to isolate some of the basic frameworks of understanding available in our society for making sense out of events and to analyze the special vulnerabilities to which these frames of reference are subjects (Goffman 1974: p.10). A frame is a definition of the situation, a perspective, that makes it possible to understand a given episode of conduct. A frame is a collective creation enabling meaningful experience. People can interpret something in situations with frames. People can also make use of frames for certain purposes (Helle 1998: pp.179-190). For example, to direct a play in order to let people review their real life or to falsify an event to lead people to fall into a trap.

There are many examples of directing a play in order to let people review their real life, for instance, a film which describes a cruel war can remind people of the old days when people killed each other. Those who have that experience may understand the film well because they have the war frame in mind. The film may have the effect to educate people to avoid wars, to strive for peace and treasure today's happy life.

There are many examples to falsify an event to lead people to fall into a trap as well, for instance, a researcher designed an experiment to test the attitude of people towards an "event". In that experiment a person of dubious character was pestering a young woman in a place where not so many people passing by. The woman was trying to run away...... One person passed without saying anything and left quickly. Two people passed by looking but seeing not. Another three people passed ...... At last, a person came up to the man and the woman to try to get rid of the man and help the woman. A video camera recorded the whole process. From the behaviour of the pedestrians, the researcher collected the data about the attitude towards that kind of phenomena in society. The frame about that phenomenon is used by the researcher. The pedestrians were led into a trap. They thought that what happened on the roadside was real, so they were feared, ignored, or felt indignant (the experiment is from a report on German television).

In the process of interaction, typically ritualized and regulated, people try to wipe away the transformed frame or to clear up the misframe in order to get back to the original primary frame, the real world (Turner 1991: pp.466-471). The question is: what is real? Back at the beginning of the dissertation, is the world of everyday life real or is the world of sacred cosmos real? Both. It depends on the individuals' frame. So during the interaction, people seek to maintain a common frame. Without a common frame, the interaction will have problems. Goffman accepts W. J. Thomas' dictum: the definition of a situation is real in its consequences. However, the statement is true as it reads but false sometimes as it is taken. He follows William James' tradition: each of the worlds has its own special and separate style of existence. The important thing about reality is our sense of its realness. He agrees Alfred Schutz's argument: instead of saying of a world that it is generated in accordance with certain structural principles, one says it has a certain cognitive style. He absorbs Harold Garfinkel's opinion: to look for rules allows us to generate a world of a given kind. So Goffman's perspective is situational, meaning here a concern for what one individual can be alive to at a particular moment. "What is it that's going on here?" when individuals attend to any current situation, they face this question. The question is put and the answer to it is presumed by the way the individuals then proceed to get on with the affairs at hand (Goffman 1974: pp.1-10).

What may be the influence of the religious beliefs on social interaction according to Goffman's theory? The frame which people have may be different because the experience which they have and the cultural environment where they live in may be different. Religious experience may have effects in a given episode of events. The immortals play a role in frame forming.

Chapter 3: Research Design

1. Investigation Method

In the history of social science, there have been three kinds of approaches which have successively occupied an important position in methodology. One approach views that social phenomena, the same as natural phenomena, have characteristics of objectivity, like the phenomena of physics, and have the characteristics of an organic whole, like the phenomena of biology. Therefore social scientific research should observe the law of natural science and put stress on objective facts. The second approach claims that human society is different from the natural world. Human beings have a consciousness and have individual differences. Therefore social scientific research is different from natural science. It should pay attention to subjective explanation. The third approach regards that human behaviours embody subjective meanings. These subjective meanings can be understood. Therefore social scientific research should try to understand the meanings of the behaviour. Understanding is the prerequisite of interpreting. Understanding can be interpreted (Yuan Fang and Wang Hansheng 1997: pp.30-38).

Different views in methodology have led to the different research methods: quantitative methods which use statistical techniques to test hypothesis; qualitative methods which use inductive methods to discover general meanings; and the combination of the quantitative and the qualitative approaches to the research methods of a study or across all phases of the research process, known as the mixed methods or mixed models (Tashakkori and Teddlie 1998: pp.17-19). Though there are differences between quantitative research and qualitative research (See Figure 7, Neuman 1994: p.317), they are two reasoning processes of one research cycle, the cycle of scientific methodology (See Figure 8,

Tashakkori and Teddlie 1998: p.25). More and more social scientists have realized that both quantitative research and qualitative research are needed in social studies. A common expression which expounds the combination of the two approaches is "to see through the appearance to get at the essence". This is also the effort of the research in this dissertation.

Figure 7: Differences Between Quantitative Research and Qualitative Research

Quantitative Research	Qualitative Research
• Test hypothesis that the researcher begins with	• Discover meaning when the researcher deals with the data
• Concepts are in the form of distinct variables	• Concepts are in the form of themes, motifs, generalizations, taxonomies
• Measures are created before data collection and are standardized	• Measures are created in an ad hoc manner and are often specific
• Data are in the form of numbers from precise measurement	• Data are in the form of words from documents, observations, transcripts
• Theory is largely causal and is deductive	• Theory can be causal or noncausal and is often inductive
• Research procedures are standard, and replication is assumed	• Research procedures are particular, and replication is rare
• Analysis proceeds by statistics and see if it relates to hypotheses	• Analysis proceeds by extracting themes or gerneralization from evidence

1.1 Questionnaire and Interview

Both questionnaire and interview are adopted in this investigation. The questionnaire and the interview outline are developed on the basis of the theme and the assumptions of the dissertation (See Chapter 2, Section 1).

Questionnaire and interview cannot peplace one another in this research because the goal of the investigation is to get the information not only extensively but also intensively. Different research needs different investigation methods. Census is a typical research which requires extensive information. Belief or interaction involves psychological mystery or complex process which requires both intensive information and extensive information.

Figure 8: Cycle of Scientific Methodology

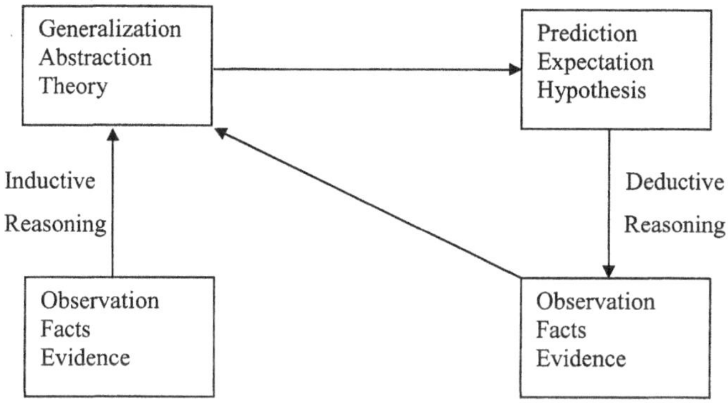

For example, in my research, I asked people "Being a stranger in a place which you do not know, how do you usually associate with others at the beginning?" Most people answered: "to get close to others" rather than "to keep distance to others". It is not too difficult to get this information from a large group of people by a questionnaire. What does it mean? It means that many people do not keep themselves alone when they are in a new place. What else does it mean? When the same question was raised in the interviews, people answered: "first look around, then find someone interesting, then see how it develops", "I simply go to them, open and friendly", "I know them naturally when I have to contact them". Those answers tell us how people get close to others: step by step, straightforward, or naturally. More answers were: "I talk to those who are friendly and sympathetic", "Who I talk to depends on how he behaves and how interesting he is", "I talk to those who makes me feel comfortable". Those answers tell us what kind of people they get to close: it depends on both the people's taste and the behaviour of the opposite side. Even more answers were obtained: "to contact others, I may learn a lot", "to know others in order to get help", "say hello to others so as not to be lonely", "to talk with others, I can get information", "to get close to others to know the people and the culture". Those answers tell us why people get close to others: to fulfill certain needs. The information from the interviews is difficult to get from a questionnaire. The information from the interviews is meaningful and useful for the research as well.

Questionnaire

The title of the questionnaire is "Beliefs and Behaviour in Everyday Life". It is different from the title of the dissertation "The influence of Religious Beliefs on Social Interaction". The word "religious" did not appeare in the questionnaire because the purpose of the investigation rather than the purpose of the dissertation was to know the people's beliefs including religious and non religious. The term "beliefs" in the questionnaire just confirms to the requirements. The word "interaction" was not used in the investigation because it seemed difficult to understand by ordinary people. The term "behaviour" is easy to understand and contains the meaning of interaction. The questionnaire was administered two languages, English and Chinese.

The questionnaire was delivered by the researcher directly to the research objects (people who accepted the investigation) and was filled by those objects. Besides a letter for the research objects and directions for filling in the form, the questionnaire contained two parts: personal data and 24 closed questions, the multiple choice (See Appendix 1).

The content of the questionnaire was the questions investigating people's beliefs and their interactions. More precisely, it was designed to investigate what people think about the immortals, for example, ancestors or god, in the beyond; how people interact with each other in everyday life, with strangers or intimates; and in addition, how people deal with problems and attribute problems in everyday life (See Chapter 3, Section 2).

Interview

The topic of the interview is the same as the topic of the questionnaire. The interviews were conducted face to face, one by one, and well structured. An interview outline was prepared. It was also applied in two languages, English and Chinese. It contained 21 open questions and an extra question which the interviewees may answer freely. These questions were raised in the same way and in the same order in each of the interviews. A tape recorder was used during the interviews (See Appendix 2).

The content of the interview was also an investigation of people's beliefs and their interactions. It was designed to be compatible with the questionnaire. The only difference between the interview outline and the questionnaire was that there were two additional questions in the interview outline: the question relating to the process of the individual's belief development, and the question about the identity of people's religious membership. At the end, an extra question was raised: Do you have some questions to ask me? They are allowed to ask any questions, the questions about what they want to know or what they want to discuss (See Chapter 3, Section 2).

1.2The Sample and the Cases

In this research, sampling survey was adopted in combination with the questionnaire and the interview. How to select smaller cases from larger pool to issue the questionnaire and how to select still smaller cases to interview was an important step. Before we discuss about the sampling and the cases, it is necessary to define a few basic concepts. (1) Sampling Element: It is the unit of analysis or case in a population. The element in this research was a person. (2) Research Population: It is a large pool of cases with a specified unit being sampled, at a specifec geographical location, and within time boundaries. The research population in this research were the Germans and the Chinese between the age of 25 and 55 years old in Munich Germany in 2003. (3) Target Population: It is a specific pool of cases which need to be investigated. Research population is a theoretical pool of cases. Target population cannot be the all because there are always some exceptions in practice. For instance, in this research, the investigation was done in English and Chinese, those who do not know English or Chinese, even though their other conditions match the investigation, could not be included. (4) Sampling Frame: It is a list of cases which can be sampled possibly. Because the boundary of the target population was not quite clear in this research, the way of sampling was a non probability sampling, it was difficult to choose a sampling frame. It was omitted (Neuman 1994: pp.193-196).

The Sample

Just now the research population and the target population were introduced. One point that needs to be mentioned is the types of cases in the research population. According to the theme of the dissertation, the cases were mainly divided into two types: people who have religious beliefs and people who do not have religious beliefs. How can we distinguish the two groups of people in the investigation? Should it depend on the people's self identity or depend on the definition in the dissertation? It depended on the people's self identity because it was difficult to know what people really believe beforehand. It can be known only after the data has been analysed. In fact, nobody was asked about his or her religious beliefs when they agreed to fill a questionnaire. However a rough percentage of people in each group could be known immediately after the data was collected. It was helpful because the researcher could make a proper adjustment among the target population during the process of the investigation.

The other point that needs to be mentioned is the age of the cases in the research population. The age of the people in this research was limited between 25 to 55 years old out of two considerations: One is the maturation of thoughts. It was supposed that people who are over 25 years old are relatively mature in thoughts. If people are young, they are easily influenced by all kinds of factors around them. Their thoughts may be changeable. What they think today may differ from what they think tomorrow. The data concerning to this research collected from them may not be very reliable. If people are old comparing with those who are just 20 or 30, their life experience is quite different from the younger generation, their thoughts may deviate from the younger people's by a lot. It makes the analysis more complicated. Another consideration is the probability of communication. The investigation was done in English and Chinese. English, needless to say Chinese, are not the native languages of the Germans. It is possible that the very young Germans and the very old Germans may have some difficulties expressing their ideas in English. It is possible that there are more probabilities of finding those to communicate among the people who are between the age of 25 and 55 years old. The general principle of sampling is to minimize the differences and to maximize the probabilities.

The Cases

The way of the sampling was a non probability sampling. This way was chosen because the individuals' information was not sufficient. For instance, it was difficult for the researcher to go to the agencies which are in charge of personal administration to get relevant information. One possible way to do was to communicate with ordinary people to ask their help. A few investigation methods were used in this research: to use quota sampling to keep the number of the cases in each category roughly the same, religious versus nonreligious, the Germans versus the Chinese; to use purposive sampling to look for cases who are supposed more religious, such as the people belonging to a religious group; to use haphazard sampling and snowball sampling to get as many cases as possible (See Chapter 3, Section 3).

The cases of the interview were selected from the sample. That means the people who are the Germans and the Chinese between the age of 25 and 55 years old in Munich, to be more important, who would like to both fill the questionnaire and accept the interview (See Chapter 3, Section 3).

1.3 The Process of the Investigation

The investigation started in the end of December, 2002. It lasted two months. It was conducted in Munich, Germany. The questionnaires were delivered and collected mainly by the researcher (the writer of the dissertation) in a derect way, assistantly by email and by the help of friends rolling snowball. The interviews were done by the researcher in the way of face to face, one by one, and well structured. The two kinds of data were collected at the same time, it was done alternately. Two languages were used in the investigation, English and Chinese. (See Chapter 3, Section 3).

2. Operational Concept and Assumption

Going back to the title of the dissertation: The Influence of Religious Beliefs on Social Interaction, the terms religious beliefs and social interaction were discussed in a previous chapter (See Chapter 2, Section 2 & 3). It may be repeated briefly. Religious beliefs in this dissertation refer to the beliefs in immortals, to be more exact, the presence of immortals in the beyond. Social interaction in this dissertation refers to the individuals acting on each other by the way of face to face contact. The term influence may be reflected from the differences between the people who have religious beliefs and the people who do not have religious beliefs in social interaction (See Chapter 2, Section 4). These concepts are clear but abstract. They need to be more concretized if a survey is carried out. The process of changing an abstract concept into measurable variables and changing a research hypothesis into concrete hypothesis is called operationalization.

2.1 Operational Concept

The beliefs in immortals in the beyond mean that there is a world in the beyond. People will live in that world after they leave this world. The "early" citizens of that world are their ancestors or a god (according to their beliefs), then themselves, then their descendants. What will the situation be if the population of immortals in that world increases unlimitedly? The question which is raised in this world will not be a question in that world because the space in that world is infinite, the time of the citizens' life is eternal. It is a supernatural being's life in a sacred cosmos.

The interaction between individuals by the way of face to face contact refers to the interaction between strangers and between intimates. It may be a general interaction under normal conditions like two strangers having an encounter in a working place or two lovers living together in a family. It may also be a particular communication in a specific situation, for example, a human and immortal communicating in a certain situation or two persons communicating with the presence of immortals in the situation.

The influence of religious beliefs on social interaction can be presented in people's general interaction or a particular communication. Does someone experience ultimate reality in interaction? For example, the immortal's images may flash before one's eyes, the immortal's words may ring in one's ears...... Or does someone interpret his experience religiously? For example, someone may attribute his turning a disadvantage into an advantage one to God's arrangement or someone may attribute a happy encounter to fate...... Of course, some of the interaction can be described while some of the interaction can only be sensed. There is a Chinese word: "It can be sensed but not explained in words".

2.2 Operational Assumptions

The basic assumptions are: people who have religious beliefs may have something in common in social interaction; people who have religious beliefs may have something different from the people who do not have religious beliefs in social interaction; it is possible that the fact in reality may contradict the first two assumptions (See Chapter 2, Section 1).

On the one hand, because religious believers have common beliefs about death and life after death, their knowledge about time, space and their knowledge about people's life or lives may be different from the non religious believers. These differences in beliefs may influence people during social interactions, the interactions with strangers and intimates. It may influence their attitude and behaviour while dealing with problems in everyday life. If people believe that life is eternal, they may do everything relatively unhurriedly. If people believe that there will be retribution, they may try to do something good. If people worship ancestors or god, they may pay a debt of gratitude. If people believe that ancestors or god gives life, they may not regard themselves or their children as their own property. If people believe in fate, they may hold themselves aloof from the world.

On the other hand, though society endows its members role expectations, the role expectations connected with a status are not fully detailed. Individuals who hold statuses may have their own orientations toward the role. They may not play their roles by passively conforming to norms but actively creating actions, to examine others and present themselves not to be hedged in by rules but breaking with conventions and tugging bold innovations (according to R. H. Turner's question about structural theory, J. H. Turner 1991: 425-427).

In addition, though members of a society possess a social position, the expectations are from all around, not only from, for example, religion, but also from other directions. Individuals who have religious beliefs (not referring to Catholic brothers and sisters or Buddhist monks and nuns) may not have a precise design of their action except that they observe religious taboos. They seem the same as those who do not have religious beliefs in working places and families except that they perform in the church. They may just have a general "gestalts" (according to R. H. Turner's question about structural theory, J. H. Turner 1991: 425-427).

Further more, though people play their roles by combining a situation, the role is not immutable or predetermined. Individuals negotiate which roles they are going to play in a situation. The situation itself can be changed, especially when a society experiences a social transition. With a changed structure, the transformed mechanism, the adjusted benefit, the new concepts, individuals' behaviour patterns, life styles and value systems will be changed as well (according to R. H. Turner's question about structural theory, J. H. Turner 1991: 425-427).

In general, the common characteristics of the religious believers in social interaction may not be obvious. The different characteristics between the religious and others may not be obvious. People may not play the roles that the religious or a certain group prescribed. Conversely, they prefer to enact roles more depending on their own interpretations of the expectations.

3. The Process of Data Collection

The sources of the data were mainly from the questionnaires and the interviewing. Both the questionnaires and the interviewing were conducted two languages, English and Chinese. With the German people, the English language was used. With the Chinese people, the Chinese language was used. The two kinds of data were collected at the same time, it was done alternately.

3.1 The Data from Questionnaire

The questionnaires were delivered and collected mainly by the researcher in a direct way, assistantly by email and by the help of friends rolling snowball. The researcher successively went to the German Catholic Church, German Buddhism Union, German Hinduism Society, Chinese Catholic Society, Chinese Christian Society, Chinese Buddhism Society, McDonald, cafeteria, bar, dining hall and Chinese School to deliver and collect the questionnaires. All those who happened to meet with the research, understood English or Chinese, were over

25 years old and were willing to fill in the questionnaire were the target. The rest of the questionnaires were collected from my acquaintances and friends, my friends' friends, their relatives, neighbours, colleagues and classmates.

The number of the delivered questionnaires was about 250 copies including the copies sent by email. The collected questionnaires were 233 copies. The valid questionnaires were 209 copies: 66 from German religious people (according to their self report), 43 from German non religious people, 44 from Chinese religious people (also according to their self report), and 56 from Chinese non religious people. The invalid questionnaires, 24 copies, were those which were not complete, filled by people from other countries, filled by people younger than 25 years old and older than 55 years old, or were collected too late to count. One matter which needs to be mentioned here is that there was a German version of the questionnaire translated by a very kind friend voluntarily. It was a pity that it was not used in the end because the translation was not accurate and it would possibly increase the difficulties in data analysis.

3.2 The Data from Interviewing

The interviews were conducted face to face, one by one, and well structured. An interview outline was prepared. It was translated into two languages, English and Chinese, to interview the German people in English and to interview the Chinese people in Chinese. The questions were raised in the same way and in the same order in each of the interviews. A tape recorder was used during the interviewing. All those who would like to both fill the questionnaire and accept the interview were welcomed. An appointment was made in advance between the interviewer and the interviewees. For the interviewees' convenience, the interviews were done in the interviewees' working places, their homes, the research's small apartment, cafeterias, or restaurants.

The number of the interviews were 32 persons: 8 were German religious people (according to their own report), 9 were German non religious people, 8 were Chinese religious people (according to their own report as well), and 7 were Chinese non religious people. All of them were interviewed by the researcher.

4. The Method of Data Analysis

Data analysis can be divided into two kinds: quantitative data analysis and qualitative data analysis. Quantitative data analysis is a method of getting information from a group of units, making a statistical analysis, and testing a hypothesis. Quantitative data are full of numbers representing values of variables which measure characteristics of research objects. Qualitative data analysis is a method of making inductive use of the data, categorizing and comparing the data, then summarizing the characteristics of the matter. Qualitative data are in the form of words describing people, actions, events in social life.

W. Lawrence Neuman makes a comparison between the two analyses (Neuman 1994: p.405) pointing out that quantitative data analysis differs from quantitative data analysis in four ways. First, quantitative analysis adopts standardized techniques. Hypothesis testing and statistical methods are very little across different social research. Qualitative analysis is less standardized. Many approaches to data analysis are matched with variety of qualitative research. Second, quantitative researchers do not begin data analysis until they have collected all of the data and condensed them into numbers. Qualitative researchers can begin data analysis early in a research while they are still collecting data. The early data analysis guide subsequent data collection. Third, quantitative researchers use numbers that represent empirical facts in order to test a hypothesis with variable constructs. Qualitative researchers create new concepts and theories by blending together empirical evidence and abstract concepts. Forth, quantitative analysis is clothed in statistics, hypothesis, and variables. The researchers use numbers to discuss causal relations. Qualitative analysis is less abstract than statistical analysis. The data are in the form of words which can have more than one meaning.

In this research, both quantitative and qualitative analysis is used. The data from the questionnaires are analysed by quantitative analysis. The data from the interviewing are analysed by qualitative analysis. By combining the two methods of analysis and comparing the results from the two kinds of analysis, a reasonable explanation may be found.

4.1 Quantitative Analysis

One purpose of data analysis in this research is to give a description of the people, their beliefs and their interactions. What do they believe, in terms of religion? How do they interact with each other, similarly or differently? According to the need of the research, a basic statistical technique is selected, frequency distributions. The statistical results are presented in the form of bivariate tables.

4.2 Qualitative Analysis

Another purpose of data analysis in this research is to give an explanation of the people, to explain their beliefs and their interactions. Why or why not do they have religious beliefs? Why do they interact with each other in a certain way? Do their self given identities of religion conform to the concept of religion in this dissertation? How do they interpret others and themselves? Are there any differences between the people who identified themselves as religious and the people who are categorized as religious according to the concept of religion in this research in social interaction? Are there any differences between people who are religious and who are not religious in social interaction? There are several methods of qualitative data analysis, for example, analytic comparison which includes the method of agreement and the method of difference, ideal type which is used in two ways to contrast the impact of contexts and as analogy.

Analytic comparison was developed by the British scholar John Stuart Mill. His method of agreement and method of difference form the basis of analytic comparison in qualitative data analysis. The method of agreement focuses a researcher's attention on what is common across cases: to establish that cases have a common outcome, then to locate a common cause, although other features of the cases may differ. The method proceeds by a process of elimination: to eliminate features as possible causes if they are not shared across cases that have a common outcome. The method of difference is a double application of the method of agreement: first to locate cases that are similar in many respects but differ in a few crucial ways, to pinpoint features whereby a set of cases are similar with regard to an outcome and causal features, and another set whereby they differ on outcomes and causal features. The method of difference reinforces information from positive cases (cases having common characters) with negative cases (cases lacking common characters) (Neuman 1994: pp.413-415).

Ideal type was developed by the German sociologist Max Weber. It is also used by many qualitative researchers. Ideal types are models or mental abstractions of social relations or processes. They are pure standards against which the data or reality can be compared. An ideal type is a device used for comparison because no reality ever fits an ideal type. Qualitative researchers have used ideal types in two ways: to contrast the impact of contexts and as analogy. Researchers who adopt an interpretive approach may use ideal types to interpret data in a way that is sensitive to the contest and cultural meanings of members. They do not test hypotheses or create a generalizable theory, but use the ideal type to bring out the specifics of each case and to emphasize the impact of the unique contest. They make contrasts between contexts often choose cases with dramatic contrasts or distinctive features. Ideal types are used as analogies to organize qualitative data. An analogy is a statement that two objects, processes, or events are similar to each other. Researchers use them to communicate ideas and to facilitate logical comparisons. Analogies transmit information about patterns in data by referring to something that is already known to the reader. Analogies can describe relationships buried deep within many details (Neuman 1994: pp.416-418).

5. Comments on the Investigation

It is necessary to say a few words about the language and the sample of the investigation. Though making effort, there are some limitations which could be done better in other research if it is possible.

5.1 About Language

The languages which were used in the investigation were English and Chinese, to investigate German people in English and to investigate Chinese people in Chinese. Two questions may be asked about the languages which were used: Are you sure that the two kinds of languages can express exactly the same meaning? Are you sure that the people from the two countries understand the questions in exactly the same way? These two questions may be raised not only in this research but also in other cross-culture research. For example, similar questions arise about the IQ tests.

In this research, in order to bridge the language gap, two ways may be used: one is to test content validity of the questionnaire and interview outline; the other is to investigate people face to face. In the first way, a small pre-survey was made, to issue the questionnaire to a small range, in this case ten German people and ten Chinese people. In the second way, multiple "techniques" were adopted, for example, to ask people to fill out the questionnaires by interview or by telephone. They could ask questions if they were not clear about the meaning of the words. Because the time of the research was short, it was necessary to make some judgments while doing. The advantage and also the disadvantage at the same time of the research was that most of the investigation objects (people who filled the questionnaires or were interviewed) were well-educated which reduced the probability of misunderstanding.

5.2 About the Sample

The scale of the sample was not large (209 cases). The way of sampling was a way of non-probability, to use a few non-probability methods together. Therefore the sample seemed not very representative. The scale of the sample and the way of sampling in this research was chosen mainly out of two considerations or limitations. The first one is the uniqueness of the research objects: the Germans and the Chinese who have religious beliefs and who do not have religious beliefs, who can understand English or Chinese. If a probability sampling was adopted, it would also need the research objects to be selected at random. This leads the second issue, the limitations of the researcher's social network. If the researcher could have had the cooperation of administrators of related agencies, adopting a probability sampling would be possible. This may be a pity. But once the research began by multiple ways, with much help from many people, a small but valuable sample was formed.

Chapter 4: Results from Questionnaire

The results from the questionnaire are divided into several subjects. Each of the subjects contains a description of the results, a table of statistics, a comparison of the results, and the questions which will be discussed in the next parts. The statistical data was from computer using SPSS software. The total research objects are categorized into four groups: German religious group, German non religious group, Chinese religious group, and Chinese non religious group. For each of the tables, a general result (result from 209 cases) and a group result (result from the 4 groups) will be displayed. A general description of the 209 cases and a comparison among the 4 groups will be shown. The words which are used in the description and comparison are: about 10% is defined as small number; about 30% is defined as some; about 50% is half; above 70% is defined as most. One point that needs to be mentioned is that the religious versus the non religious are distinguished by the people's self given identity (the answer of the item on religious belief in the questionnaire); The Germans versus the Chinese are distinguished by the people's country of origin (the answer of the item on country origin in the questionnaire).

1. Personal Data

The general description of the people who filled the questionnaire is: The proportion of the religious and the non religious is roughly equal, the religious account for 52.6% and the non religious account for 47.4%. The proportion of the Germans and the Chinese is roughly equal, the Germans make up 52.2% and the Chinese make up 47.8%. The proportion of the male and the female is also roughly equal, each of them amount to 52.6% and 47.4%. About the age of them, 95.2% of them are between 25-45 years old, only 4.3% are over 45. As to the other aspects, 49.8% of them are single and 46.4% are married. 34.0% of them have children and 65.6% of them have not. 85.6% of them have university education and only 13.9% have not. Most of them are working, that accounts for 62.2%, some of them are studying, which accounts for 26.3%. Most of them think that they have sufficient income, which amounts to 61.7%, some of them think it insufficient, that amounts to 27.3% (See Table 1).

Table 1: Personal Data

	German Religious	German non Religious	Chinese Religious	Chinese non Religious	General
Male	53.0	60.5	52.3	46.4	52.6
Female	47.0	39.5	47.7	53.6	47.4
25-35	59.1	67.4	63.6	55.4	60.8
36-45	36.4	23.3	34.1	41.1	34.4
46-55	3.0	9.3	2.3	3.6	4.3
Single	65.2	65.1	34.1	32.1	49.8
Married	30.3	30.2	61.4	66.1	46.4
Divorced	4.5	4.7	4.5	1.8	3.8
No Uni Edu	18.2	20.9	15.9	1.8	13.9
Have Uni Edu	80.3	79.1	84.1	98.2	85.6
Study	18.2	23.3	29.5	35.7	26.3
Work	68.2	69.8	56.8	53.6	62.2
Home	3.0	2.3	9.1	5.4	4.8
Insufficient	28.8	25.6	18.2	33.9	27.3
Sufficient	59.1	53.5	75.0	60.7	61.7
Surplus	9.1	14.0	0	0	5.7
No Children	78.8	83.7	47.7	50.0	65.6
Have Children	21.2	16.3	50.0	50.0	34.0
Missing	11	5	6	6	28

Comparing the four groups, the differences between the German religious and the German non religious in each of the variables are not obvious. The quantitative differences are less than 10%. The differences between the Chinese religious and the Chinese non religious, in general, are not obvious. Only on the aspects of education and income there are some differences. The percentage of having university education among the Chinese religious are lower than the Chinese non religious and the percentage of income sufficient among the Chinese religious are higher than the Chinese non religious. The differences between the Germans and the Chinese are obvious in some aspects. The percentage of the people who get married among the Germans are lower than the Chinese, 30.3% versus 64.0%. The percentage of the people who have children among the Germans are lower than the Chinese, 19.3% versus 50.0%. In addition, the percentage of the people who have university education are quite high both among the Germans and among the Chinese, 79.8% and 92.0%.

One point that needs to be explained here is that, besides the data of the three variables, people's religious beliefs, country of origins, and their age were controlled during the process of data collection by using quota sampling and purposive sampling in order to be sure that the number of the cases in each category was roughly equal. Other data of other variables were obtained by random. The other point that needs to be explained is that the percentage of having university education is quite high because higher education in Germany is relatively universal, most of the Chinese who come to Germany by entering a university first. The largest group of the Chinese in Munich is the group of the university students. The language which is used in the investigation determined those who may have university education. Of course, the German language and the English language belong to one family of Latin. It is more general among the Germans than among the Chinese that they know English.

2. Beliefs in Death and Life after Death

Beliefs in death and life after death in the questionnaire are asked by the questions "What does it mean when your body is dead? Does it mean a turning point of life or terminal point of life when your body is dead?" and "Where will you go after your body is dead? Is there still a place for continue living or only the graveyard for eternal sleep after your body is dead?" Then the further questions relating to the first two questions are "Does one have opportunities to deal with things and to fulfil his desires in the hereafter or does one have no opportunities later if one cannot do what one wants today?" and "Will one receive the reward or punishment for his good or bad behaviour today in the next life or does it have no relationship between what he does now and in the hereafter?"

It is supposed that people who have religious beliefs may think that the death of a body is a turning point of life. They can go to another place living in another form after the death of a body. They might continue fulfilling their desires hereafter. And they will receive the reward or punishment in the next life. People who do not have religious beliefs may think the opposite. Is it possible that some people may have a third kind of opinions? Yes. It is possible that they have and it is possible for them to express their opinions anyway according to the design of the questionnaire, to choose the answer "other" then explain it (See Table 2 and 3, Table 4 and 5).

2.1 Beliefs in Death

The investigation results from Table 2 and 3 show that some people believe that death is a turning point of life and they will go to another place living in another form after the death of a body. They answered questions religiously according to

Table 2: Beliefs in Death (1)

	German Religious	German non Religious	Chinese Religious	Chinese non Religious	General
Turning Point	56.1	16.3	65.9	10.7	37.8
Terminal Point	22.7	53.5	13.6	78.6	42.1
Other	21.2	30.2	20.5	10.7	20.1

Missing Cases = 0

Table 3: Beliefs in Death (2)

	German Religious	German non Religious	Chinese Religious	Chinese non Religious	General
Another Place	53.0	23.3	56.8	17.9	38.3
Graveyard	13.6	23.3	9.1	51.8	24.9
Other	31.8	53.5	31.8	30.4	35.9

Missing Cases = 2

the supposition of the dissertation. Some people think that death is a terminal point of life and they will go to the graveyard and sleep under the ground after the death of a body. They answered the questions non religiously. And some people gave the third kind of answers. Comparing the four groups, more than half of the people in both the German religious group and the Chinese religious group answered the questions religiously (according to the basic concept of religion in the dissertation) and more than half of the people in both the German non religious group and the Chinese non religious group answered questions non religiously (according to the basic concept of religion in the dissertation) except the German non religious group in the second question in which the percentage of the people who believe that they will go to the graveyard after death is not high. They gave their own answers. Some people in each group gave the answers which do not conform to the supposition of the research according to their own belief identities. It means that some people have the identity of being a religious but did not answer the questions religiously while some people have the identity of being non religious but answered the questions religiously.

What are the other answers? They can also be categorized into religious, non religious and the third kind. The beliefs are religious because they contain the meanings that the death of the body does not mean the death of life and that there will be life after death. Examples of these beliefs are: "Life will continue totally in a different way after death", "Body is dead but the mind stream rebirth in another form", "There will be a resurrection or reincarnation after death", "My body died but my soul will exist", "Death in this world means birth in another", "I will go to heaven or paradise after death", "I will go to Jesus because he saved me in this earth". The beliefs are not religious because they contain the meanings which are opposite to the religious beliefs. For example: "Death is the end and no place to go", "I will disappear forever", "I will go back to nature", "Nothing will happen when I die". The third kind of answers are neither religious nor non religious because they contain the meaning of not knowing, or not being sure, or wanting to know. For example: "I don't know", "I cannot answer it", "How can I know it?", "I am not sure about it", "I never thought about it", "Who can tell me that?", "I would really like to know". Half of the people in the German non religious group gave their own answers about where they will go after death. Those answers are either the second type or the third type. The people's own explanations illustrate that the percentage of the religious and the non religious is not limited to the numbers of selecting the given answers. Though some people did not select the given answers in the questionnaire, they expressed their ideas in their own way. Regardless what words they used, the meanings are clear as either religious or non religious from the view of understanding them.

2.2 Life after Death

The investigation results from Table 4 and 5 show that not so many people believe that one will have opportunities to continue doing what he is doing today in the hereafter and more than half of the people believe that one will not have that opportunity. Some people think that there will be retribution in the next life but it amounts to less than those who think the opposite. Again, there are some people who gave a third kind of answer. Comparing the four groups, the percentage of those who think that one will have opportunities to do what he wants in the hereafter is lower than the opposite side in each group. It is even lower in the two non religious groups. The percentage of those who believe that there will be a reward or punishment in the hereafter for his good or bad behaviour today is not high in the two religious groups but it is higher than the opposite side of the same groups and it is much higher than in the two non religious groups. It is low in the two non religious groups. It seems that the absolute percentage of those in the religious groups whose answers conform to the supposition of the dissertation is not obvious high but the relative percentage of it is obvious high. Again, some people in each group gave the answers which do not conform to the supposition of the research according to their own belief identities.

What are the other answers? They can be again categorized into religious, non religious and the third kind. The answers are religious because they contain the meanings that there is a certain relationship between the life in this world and the life in the next though life in the next world may differ from life now. Examples of those answers are: "I will become another person and have other

Table 4: Life after Death (1)

	German Religious	German non Religious	Chinese Religious	Chinese non Religious	General
Continue	19.7	11.6	27.3	8.9	16.7
Not Continue	57.6	65.1	47.7	82.1	63.6
Other	21.2	23.3	25.0	7.1	18.7

Missing Cases = 2

Table 5: Life after Death (2)

	German Religious	German non Religious	Chinese Religious	Chinese non Religious	General
Retribution	37.9	4.7	45.5	25.0	29.2
No Retribution	30.3	48.8	22.7	62.5	41.1
Other	31.8	46.5	31.8	12.5	29.7

Missing Cases = 0

interests", "Life will be in another form, people will do another kind of things", "Next life depends on the consequences of this life", "It is a matter of cause and effect", "God will forgive you not punish you", "Do good things in this life then reward will be great", "God will make a judgement for you". Their answers are not religious because they contain the meanings that are opposite to the above answers. For example: "One can only do something on earth then no chance", "The reward or punishment just in this actual life", "Life is over quiet unexpectedly", "It doesn't matter since I'm dead", "This life is limited so do as much as you can", "One doesn't do anything after this life", "To fulfil my desires depends on my descendants". The third answers convey the idea of not knowing or not being sure. For example: "I don't know", "I am not sure", "Life is eternal but one can only do things on earth then no chance", "No hereafter but work seems forever", "I never thought about it", "I don't know what will be but do well in this life", "Life is eternal but I don't know if I can continue doing the work in the next life", "It depends if he has a belief", "It's an issue of psychology".

2.3 Small Summary

A small summary of the results is: (1) Most people in the two religious groups believe that death is a turning point of life and they can go on living in another place and in another form after death. Most people in the two non religious groups believe that death is a terminal point of life and they can only go to the graveyard and sleep eternally after death. It means that their self given identities of being religious or non religious conform to the supposition of the dissertation. (2) Not so many people in the two religious groups believe that they can continue what they are doing today in the hereafter but some people believe that there will be retribution in the hereafter. Consulting their own answers, some of them may not believe they can continue what they are doing today in the hereafter but they can continue doing something else in the hereafter. Most people in the two non religious groups believe that there will be no opportunities to do anything and no retribution hereafter. It means that their self given identity of being religious or non religious is not contradictory with the supposition of the dissertation. (3) There are a small number of people, in general 10%-20% in each group, whose self given identities are religious or non religious but who answered the questions in a way which contradicts the supposition of the dissertation about being religious or non religious. (4) There are some people or many people in some groups who gave other answers. Among those people, most of them expressed clear meanings which can be understood as being religious or non religious. But some of them show that beliefs in their mind are uncertainty, confusion, or contradiction.

The questions are: (1) Many people have a common belief that death of a body is not the end of life but not so many people have a common belief that there will be a continuity of what they are doing today in the hereafter though they believe that they can continue doing something. What will be the life after death? (2) Some people identify themselves as religious or non religious but their beliefs seem contradictory according to the supposition of the dissertation about being religious or non religious. What are the concepts of religion for them? (3) Some people showed their uncertainty, confusion or contradiction in beliefs. What does it result from and result in?

3. Relationship Between the Living and the Dead

Relationship between the living and the dead in the questionnaire are asked by the questions "What do you think about your dead relatives? Are they still living somewhere or have they disappeared from this world?" and "Do your dead relatives sometimes appear in front of you? Is it a reality that they really come to you or is it a fantasy that you just think of them?" Then the further questions are "Our ancestors or god (if you believe) gave us life, do they have power to dominate us in this world or do they have no power because they are gone or never existed?" and "Our descendants will live in this world after we leave here, are they the extension of your life or are they the successors to your cause?" The questions in the preceding section are about the intrapersonal relationship between the living self today and the dead self hereafter. The questions in this section are about the interpersonal relationship between the living self and their dead ancestors and between the dead self and their living descendants.

It is supposed that people who have religious beliefs may think that their dead relatives are still living somewhere. If they have the belief, they may have the experience of encountering their dead relatives. This kind of belief or experience should show no differences from their beliefs in death and life after death because the presupposition of all these beliefs is that there are immortals in the beyond. Then it is supposed that people who have religious beliefs may think that the ancestors or God has power over them and they themselves after death will have power over their descendants. Of course, ancestors are different from God because some people said that ancestors did live in this world and ancestors were created by God. But if people believe either ancestors or God are the immortals in the beyond and worship them, there will be no difference. People who do not have religious beliefs may think differently. A third kind of opinions is possible as well (See Table 6 and 7, Table 8 and 9).

3.1 Relationship with Dead Relatives

The investigation results from Table 6 show that some people believe that their dead relatives are still living somewhere. Some people believe that their dead relatives disappeared from this world. And some people gave the third kind of answers. Comparing the four groups, half or more than half of the people in the two religious groups answered the questions religiously. More than half of the people in the two non religious groups answered the questions non religiously. But some people in each group gave the answers which do not conform to the supposition of the dissertation in regards to being religious or non religious according to their own belief identities.

The investigation results from Table 7 show that there are only a small number of people in the two religious groups that have had the experience of their dead relatives appearing to them as a reality and even fewer people in the two non religious groups have had that experience. This does not certainly mean that their beliefs are contradictory because they may believe in something but may not have the same experience. Only when the people's belief reaches a certain level or people are in a certain circumstances, do they have the experience. Most people in each group believe that it is because they think of their dead relatives so much that the dead relatives seem to appear to them. Some people gave a third kind of answers. Again, some people in each group gave the answers which do not conform to the supposition of the research about being religious or non religious according to their own belief identities.

Table 6: About Dead Relatives (1)

	German Religious	German non Religious	Chinese Religious	Chinese non Religious	General
Still living	47.0	11.6	59.1	19.6	34.9
Disappeared forever	22.7	58.1	20.5	55.4	38.3
Other	30.0	30.2	20.5	25.0	26.8

Missing Cases = 0

Table 7: About Dead Relatives (2)

	German Religious	German non Religious	Chinese Religious	Chinese non Religious	General
Really Come	10.6	2.3	13.6	3.6	7.7
Think of Them	54.5	51.2	52.3	85.7	61.7
Other	33.3	46.5	31.8	10.7	29.7

Missing Cases = 2

What are the other answers? They can be categorized into religious, non religious and the third kind. The beliefs are religious because they contain the meanings that their dead relatives are immortals and they can communicate or interact with the immortals. They may have the experience that their dead relatives appearing as a divine being. For example: "They live somewhere in a totally different way", "Good ones in heaven and bad ones in hell", "They live in peace of God", "They went to Jesus", "Their spirit is there", "They are around somewhere watching me". The beliefs are not religious because they contain the meanings which are opposite to the religious beliefs while they express a feeling of cherishing the memory of the dead. For example: "They have disappeared but live in my memory", "I miss them in my mind", "They have influence over me", "I never had the experience of their appearing to me", "I cannot believe that they can come". The third kind of answers are neither religious nor non religious. For example: "I don't know", "I am not sure", "I did not think about it before", "I hope that some parts of them continue", "It is possible that they are still living".

3.2 Relationship with Ancestors and God

The investigation results from Table 8 show that some people think that the ancestors or God have power. Some people think that ancestors or God have no power. Some people gave the third kind of answers. Comparing the four groups, only some people in the German religious group believe the ancestors' or God's power while most people in the Chinese religious group believe that. Half or more than half of the people in the two non religious groups deny the ancestors or God power. More people in the two German groups than in the two Chinese groups gave other answers, especially the people in the German religious group.

What are the other answers? They can be categorized into religious, non religious and the third kind. They are religious because they contain the meanings that the human beings always have a relationship with the immortals, their ancestors or God. For example: "The humans and God live together and manipulate each other", "The ancestors have no power but God has", "God has power but not manipulate us", "They have no power but help us", "God has power but also gives us freedom". They are not religious because they contain the meanings that the immortals do not exist. The dead have no relationship with the living ones. For example: "The ancestors are dead. How can they say to us or hear from us?", "The ancestors do not exist anymore but their creations still exist", "They have the power which is created in my mind", "I have my own free will, my ancestors only influence me by their heritage". The third answers are neither religious nor non religious. For example: "I don't know, who knows?", "I am not sure, maybe it is true or maybe it is false", "Believing is effective".

Table 8: Relations with Ancestors

	German Religious	German non Religious	Chinese Religious	Chinese non Religious	General
Have Power	27.3	9.3	61.4	25.0	30.1
Have no Power	21.2	48.8	11.4	58.9	34.9
Other	50.0	39.5	20.5	16.1	32.5

Missing Cases = 5

3.3 Relationship with Descendants

The investigation results from Table 9 show that some people think that their descendants are the extension of their life, some people think that their descendants are the successors of their cause, and some people gave their own answers. Comparing the four groups, there are not many differences among the percentage of people who choose each of the answers in the two German groups but there are some differences in the two Chinese groups. The percentage of the people who think that their descendants are the extension of their life is higher than the percentage of the people who chose other answers in the two Chinese groups. More people in the two German groups than in the two Chinese groups gave other answers.

Table 9: Relations with Descendants

	German Religious	German non Religious	Chinese Religious	Chinese non Religious	General
Extension of Life	30.3	32.6	54.5	41.1	38.8
Successor of Cause	25.8	23.3	18.2	37.5	26.8
Other	37.9	41.9	20.5	17.9	29.7

Missing Cases =10

What are the other answers? They can be categorized into religious, non religious and the third kind. They are religious because they contain the meanings that the human beings always have a relationship with the immortals, first with their ancestors, then with their descendants when they themselves become the immortals but few people think that they will have the sacred characters as their ancestors or God. For example: "God gave us life and created our descendants too". "I may have relationship with my descendants after I die but it will be different from the relationship now". They are not religious because they contain the meanings that the immortals do not exist. The dead have no relationship with the living. For example: "My descendants have their own life, I pass them some of my physical properties", "My descendants are just people of their own". The third kind of answers are neither religious nor non religious. For example: "I don't know, who knows?", "I am not sure, maybe it is true or maybe it is false", "Believing is effective".

3.4 Small Summary

A small summary of the results is: (1) Most people in the two religious groups believe that their dead relatives are still living somewhere. Most people in the two non religious groups believe that their dead relatives do not exist anymore. It means that their self given identities of being religious or non religious conform to the supposition of the dissertation at this point. It also means that their beliefs in death and life after death are identical with the beliefs in their dead relatives. Though many people believe that their dead relatives are still living somewhere, few of them have the experience of communicating or interacting with them. (2) The differences between the two religious groups and the two non religious groups can be seen roughly from the question of relationship with ancestors and God. The differences are more obvious between the two Chinese groups than between the two German groups. From people's own expressions, we can see that the German religious people believe in God rather than ancestors. The image of God is as a supervisor rather than a ruler. The differences between the two religious groups and the two non religious groups are not obvious from the question of relationship with descendants. But it is obvious that the view of "extension of life" is stronger than the view of "successor of cause" in the Chinese religious group. From people's own expressions, we know that the Germans both religious and non religious think that their descendants are independent individuals rather than accessories. (3) There are a certain number of people, whose self given identities are religious or non religious but who answered the questions differently from the supposition of the dissertation about being religious or non religious. As the questions become more and more complicated, this difference cannot be simply regarded as the contradictory of the people's beliefs, more detailed research needs to be done.

(4) There are some people or many people in some groups who gave other answers. Among those people, most of them expressed their meanings clearly. But some of them show that beliefs in their mind are uncertainty, confusion, or contradiction. The answers like "I don't know", "not to be sure", "never thought", are not regarded as missing values, but are regarded as important information in this research.

The questions are: (1) Many people have a common view of the existence of immortals in the beyond but some of them have a different view of the life of immortals in the beyond and different view of interactions and relationships with immortals in the beyond. It is similar to the issues of belief in death and life after death that many people have a common belief that the death of a body is not the end of life but not so many people have a common belief that there will be a continuity of what they are doing today in the hereafter though they believe that they can continue doing something. What is the relationship between the dead and the living? (2) Some people identify themselves as religious or non religious but their beliefs concerning further questions seem contradictory again according to the supposition of the dissertation about being religious or non religious. What are the concepts of religion to them? (3) Some people showed their uncertainty, confusion or contradiction again in beliefs relating to the further questions. What does it result from and result in?

To synthesize the eight questions about the beliefs in death and life after death as well as the relationship between the living and the dead which were just discussed above, to measure the agreement of the people's concept with the concept of religion defined in the dissertation, the following results are obtained. The way of doing this is to recode the values of each question, for example, to recode the value of religious=1 and others values =0 or recode the value of non religious=1 and others=0, then to define a new variable by plus the all values of the eight questions together, then make a statistic. It shows that how many given answers as religious or non religious in the questions are agreed on by people. The more given answers as religious or non religious in the questionnaire are agreed on by people, the stronger people agree with the concept of the dissertation. The following chart and table shows the percentage of the people who agreed with the given answers of the eight questions of the questionnaire (See Chart 1 and 2) and the group scores, the average number of the given answers they agreed on in the eight questions of the questionnaire (See Table 10).

Chart 1: Recode Religious Answers as 1

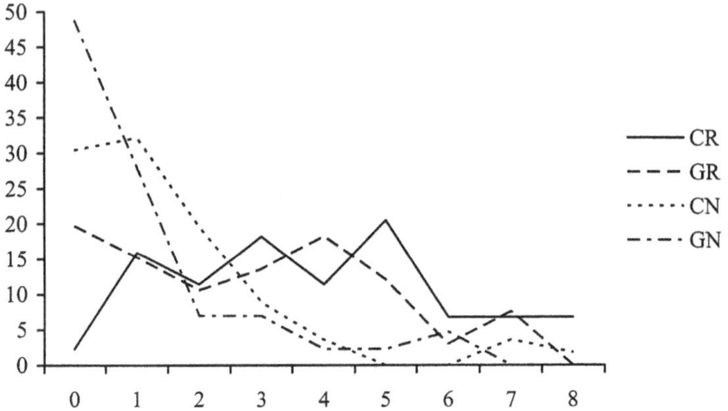

Chart 1 illustrates the tendency of the four groups, to recode the given answers which are regarded as religious according to the concept of the dissertation as "1", others answers as "0", to see what percentage of each group have on different scores. It is clear to see that the two religious groups have higher score than the two non religious groups on given answers which are regarded as religious according to the concept of the dissertation. It conforms to the supposition of the dissertation. But how much does it conform? A coordinate table is displayed in order to make a further exploration.

Chart 2: Recode Non Religious Answers as 1

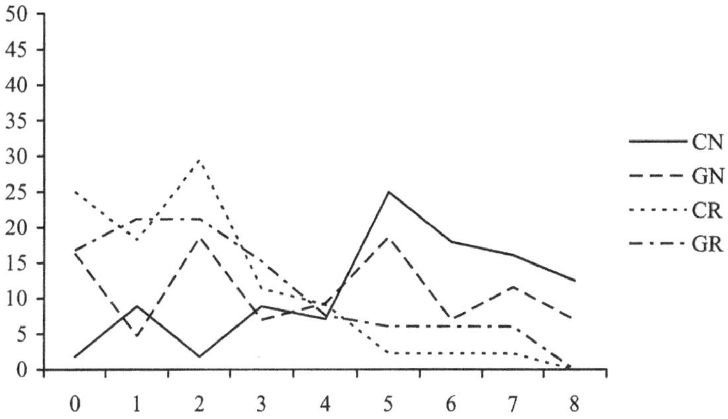

Chart 2 illustrates the tendency of the four groups as well, to recode the given answers which are regarded as non religious according to the concept of the dissertation as "1", others answers as "0", to see what percentage of each group have on different scores. It is clear to see that the two non religious groups have higher score than the two religious groups on given answers which are regarded as non religious according to the concept of the dissertation. It conforms to the supposition of the dissertation. But how much does it conform? The coordinate table is displayed in order to make a further exploration.

Table 10 shows that it shapes the same tendency as Chart 1 and Chart 2, the tendency of the four groups, to recode the given answers which are regarded as religious according to the concept of the dissertation as "1", other answers as "0", then to recode the given answers which are regarded as not religious according to the concept of the dissertation as "1", other answers as "0", to see the average number of the given answers they agreed on in the eight questions of the questionnaire. The two religious groups have higher score than the two non religious groups in the first recoding. The two non religious groups have a higher score than the two religious groups in the second recoding. To normalized to maximum score 3.84 of the first recoding and 5.13 of the second recoding, the above differences are obvious. It means that the differences in beliefs between the religious and the non religious are obvious. But the average scores in each group are not very high. Combining the results which are described in the above sections, it is because there is divergence of views on the issues of life after death though the views on death are relatively convergent, and it is also because there is divergence of views on the relationship between the living and the dead though the views on the existence of the immortals are relatively convergent. It means that the beliefs of the religious people or the beliefs of the non religious people on some aspects, not all the aspects, are not identical, especially in the two religious groups, the agreement among the religious people is less stronger than the agreement among the non religious people. The question is: What actually are the concepts of religion in people's minds?

Table 10: The Agreement with the Concept of the Dissertation

	German Religious	German Non Religious	Chinese Religious	Chinese Non Religious
Religious=1 Others=0	2.82 (average) 0.73 (normalized)	1.12 (average) 0.29 (normalized)	3.84 (average) 1 (normalized)	1.52 (average) 0.40 (normalized)
Non Religious=1 Others=0	2.48 (average) 0.48 (normalized)	3.72 (average) 0.73 (normalized)	1.89 (average) 0.36 (normalized)	5.13 (average) 1 (normalized)

4. Interaction with Strangers

Interaction with strangers in the questionnaire is asked by the questions: "If a stranger helps you on his own initiative in a place which you do not know, will you be happy and accept it or will you be upset and refuse it?" "If a newcomer joins your work or study group, will you be close to him and let him know you or will you keep distance to him and observe him?" "If you go to a new place to work or study without a person whom you know, will you be close to others and try to know others or will you keep distance to others and maintain your anonymity?" "If a newcomer makes a suggestion on your work, will you be thankful and consider it or will you be annoyed and ignore it?". These four questions imply that being a stranger in a strange place or seeing a stranger in a familiar place, a person's psychological feelings and behavioural expressions: does he or she trust others or doubt others? Does he or she get close to others or keep distance to others?

4.1 Work with Strangers

As it was discussed in the theoretical part, a regular way of social interaction in the society has been shaped over decades of life. When strangers meet each other, they usually maintain anonymity and also produce a relationship at the same time. The principle of keeping a balance between anonymity and relationship is to minimize involvement and maximize order. Though strangers typically follow this principle, some people could be warmer while some people could be colder. For example, every year there are a lot of newcomers coming to Munich from China work or study. Just setting foot on the land of a foreign country, strangeness, loneliness, even aimlessness is a normal feeling for many people. At this time, you may hear from others or it may be suggested by someone "Go to TuanQi" (the German translation means "Biblekreis"). TuanQi is a Chinese Christian Society in Munich. Every week the society has regular activities. People in that Kreis exchange ideas and share experiences. It is said that people from there are very friendly. They call each other within the society brothers and sisters. If someone has problems, he or she may get help from those people. Another similar society in Munich is Chinese Catholic Society. The priest there says to everybody every time "We hope you to have a feeling of being home here." Does this example mean that people who belong to a religious group or who participate the group's activities regularly are warmer than the others? Might be or might be not. Some people who have religious beliefs say: If everybody follows the principle of God, there will be a happy world. It teaches you to love people, to be true to people. If everybody believes in God, he will carry forward the principle of God. It is supposed that people who have religious beliefs may differ from people who do not have religious beliefs in interaction with strangers (See Table 11-14).

The investigation results from the four tables (Table 11-14) show that the overwhelming majority of people would get close to others rather than keep distance to others regardless if they themselves are strangers in a new place or they see a stranger in a familiar place. They would like to accept strangers' help and to heed to strangers' suggestions. Comparing the four groups, there are not many differences. The percentage of the people in each group might be a little bit higher on some aspects or a little bit lower on other aspects. In general, the percentage of the people in every group is high on the active aspects.

What are the other answers? In the situation of being a stranger when others offer a help, the answers are: "Accept it carefully", "See their motives and observe them", "Depends on their behaviour, friendly?", "Depends on the situation, dangerous?", "I hesitate how to do", "Hope it is helpful", "Accept but what behind?" In the situation of treating a stranger when work with him, the

Table 11: Being a Stranger When Others Help You

	German Religious	German non Religious	Chinese Religious	Chinese non Religious	General
Happy and Accept	84.8	81.4	93.2	76.8	83.7
Upset and Refuse	4.5	4.7	4.5	5.4	4.8
Other	10.6	14.0	2.3	17.9	11.5

Missing Cases = 0

Table 12: Treating a Stranger When Works with You

	German Religious	German non Religious	Chinese Religious	Chinese non Religious	General
Get Close and Know	74.2	69.8	86.4	60.7	72.2
Keep Distance and See	10.6	16.3	11.4	30.4	17.2
Other	15.2	14.0	2.3	8.9	10.5

Missing Cases = 0

answers are: "Depends on his attitude, modest?", "Depends on my impression on him", "Help him later when know each other well", "Help him if he asks me", "Depends on his behaviour, cooperate?", "Get close and observe at the same time", "Let him know me, then I will see". In the situation of being a stranger when work with others, the answers are: "First keep distance, then observe, then get close", "Neither keep distance nor get close, in between", "Get close to others step by step and more and more", "To know those who want to know me", "Depends on others, if cold, keep away", "Look for others when I have difficulties", "Keep distance out of nature, get close to others so as not to be lonely". In the situation of treating a stranger when get suggestion from him, the answers are: "Depends on how convincing his suggestion is reasonable?", "First thank for it then decide how to do", "Depends on the way he makes, politely?", "Depends on his experience, an expert?", "Give motivation to him"

Table 13: Being a Stranger When Work with Others

	German Religious	German non Religious	Chinese Religious	Chinese non Religious	General
Get Close and Know	80.3	74.4	81.8	91.1	82.3
Keep distance and alone	6.1	7.0	9.1	7.1	7.2
Other	13.6	18.6	9.1	1.8	10.5

Missing Cases = 0

Table 14: Treating a Stranger When Suggests You

	German Religious	German non Religious	Chinese Religious	Chinese non Religious	General
Thankful and Consider	74.2	74.4	86.4	91.1	81.3
Annoyed and Ignore	3.0	4.7	0	0	1.9
Other	22.7	20.9	11.4	8.9	16.3

Missing Cases = 1

4.2 Small Summary

To summarize the results: (1) The overwhelming majority of people would get close to others rather than keep distance in both the situations that they themselves are strangers in a new place or they see a stranger in a familiar place.

They would like to accept strangers' help and heed to strangers' suggestions. It seems that they trust strangers more than they doubt them. Compared with the principle of keeping balance in social interaction with strangers, it seems that the involvement is not only needed but also preferred in producing relationships. (2) There is not much difference found between the people who have religious beliefs and who do not have religious beliefs in their interactions with strangers on the aspects of the investigation. But in the Chinese non religious group, the percentage of people who interact with strangers in different situations is different. It seems that they are more initiative to get close to others when they go to a new place than when they stay in an old place. (3) Some people gave other answers, though they are small in numbers, it is nevertheless worth paying attention to. Their answers were typically "It depends". What does it depend? It depends on both sides of the interaction. It also depends on the situation of the interaction. The limitation of the questionnaire is that it is difficult to design each of the possible situations. This limitation can be broken in the parallel investigation, the interview.

The questions are: (1) Considering the principle of the balance between keeping anonymity and building relationships when strangers encounter each other, the investigation results draw forth a question: Do people prefer to increase involvement in order to build relationships because they are gregarious? Or do people need to increase involvement so as not to be alone because they are pragmatic? Or do the questions and the answers in the questionnaire imply other meanings according to people's opinions, for example, values or fashion? (2) The result from the Chinese non religious group shows that the percentage of people who interact with strangers in different situations is different. Are they the differences in the interaction by the combinations between different strangers, for example, the strangers between two Chinese in China or in Germany, a Chinese and a foreigner in China or in Germany? Or are they the differences in the interaction in different occasions, for example, in the street, in a party, in the neighbourhood, and in working place? (3) The other answers show that some people are cautious in their interactions with strangers. It seems that people observe the principle of minimizing involvement and maximizing order. But they account for less than 20% in the investigation. What is actually true?

4.3 Special Topic: Love at First Sight

To investigate the interaction between strangers, two additional questions were raised in the questionnaire: "If a man and a woman fall in love at first sight, is it because of fate or because that they attract each other?", "If two persons feel like old friends at the first meeting, is it because of fate or because they attract each other?". It is true that sometimes two persons are brought together by chance and something making them feel that they are special like lovers or friends. Some of them may explain their meeting as predestined. People normally describe the rapid development of a relationship between strangers as "flash". These two questions aim to ask people how they explain it. It is supposed that people who have religious beliefs are more likely to say that they have met each other because of predestination, for example, it is God's arrangement from the view of Christianity or it is Karma from the view of Buddhism (See Table 15 and 16).

The investigation results from Table 15 and 16 show that some people believe that falling in love at first sight and feeling like old friends at first meeting is because of fate. Most people think that it is because of attraction. Some people gave a third kind of answers. Comparing the four groups, the differences between the religious people and the non religious people are not obvious. But there are some differences between the German people and the Chinese people.

The percentage of people who believe in fate among the German people (11.9% and 14.7%) is lower than among the Chinese people (29.0% and 39.0%).

Table 15: Why Fall in Love at First Sight

	German Religious	German non Religious	Chinese Religious	Chinese non Religious	General
Fate	13.6	9.3	27.3	30.4	20.1
Attraction	68.2	67.4	65.9	60.7	65.6
Other	18.2	23.3	6.8	7.1	13.9

Missing Cases = 1

Table 16: Why Like Old Friends at First Meet

	German Religious	German non Religious	Chinese Religious	Chinese non Religious	General
Fate	13.6	16.3	34.1	42.9	26.3
Attraction	54.5	53.5	45.5	48.2	50.7
Other	31.8	30.2	20.5	8.9	23.0

Missing Cases = 0

What are the other answers? They can also be categorized into a belief in fate, to think that it is attraction, and others. Those who believe in fate wrote: "It is Karma". Those who think that it is attraction wrote: "Because they have common traits", "Because they have similar temperament", "Because they have same educational background", "Because they have similar living environment", "Because they have same interests and hobbies", and "Because of sexual attraction". The other answers are: "It needs to see special cases", "It is suspicious", "It is hard to say", "I never know the case", "I do not believe it", "Fate is a Chinese saying while attraction is a western saying".

The questions are: (1) Most people think that strangers become lovers or friends immediately because they attract each other. Why do some people fall in love at first sight while some people divorce after living together for many years? Why do some people feel like old friends at first meeting while some people know each other for a long time but fight each other often? What is or what are the key factors for people's being attracted to each other and maintaining the relationship? (2) The differences in the answers of these two questions are not obvious between the religious people and the non religious people but there are differences between the German people and the Chinese people. Some Chinese people believe in fate. What is the concept of fate from the Germans view and the Chinese view?

5. Interaction with Intimates

Interaction with intimates in the questionnaire are asked by the questions: "To contact with your partner or intimates, do you often tell him or her your private thoughts or do you often hide your private thoughts?", "To contact with your partner or intimates, do you often express your feelings to him or her or do you often control your feelings to him or her?" "To contact with your partner or intimates, are you interested in what he or she is interested or do you have your interests and he or she has his or her interests?" "To contact with your partner or intimates, do you always try to understand him or her as much as you can or do you need not understand him or her that much?". These four questions imply the meanings that to contact with partner (husband and wife, boy friend and girl friend) or with intimates (parents and children, brothers and sisters), do they share their behaviour, for example, to self disclose their thoughts, to express their feelings? do they share their experience, for example, to share their interests, to understand each other?"

5.1 Share with Intimates

It is supposed that an intimate relationship between people is established by the intimate behaviour. It does not make a supposition beforehand that there are differences between the religious people and the non religious people. But sometimes people may talk about intimate behaviour and intimate relationship, talk about what happened around them. People sometimes attribute it to religion because some good examples they can see are among the religious people. In addition, the people who have religious beliefs may be influenced not only by secular morals and ethics but also by religious morals and ethics. They keep themselves within the double bounds. The people who belong to a religious society, are educated to love both God and man. In this sense, it could be supposed that people who have religious beliefs are more possible to associate with each other intimately than the people who do not have religious beliefs (See Table 17-20).

The investigation results from the four tables (Table 17-20) show that most people have intimate interactions with their partners or their intimates, to lay bare their thoughts, to express their feelings, to share their interests, and to understand others. Comparing the four groups, the differences between the religious people and the non religious people are not significant. But the differences between the German people and the Chinese people can be found. The percentage of the people who are positive about the four aspects in the two German groups is higher than in the two Chinese groups, especially on the aspects of disclosing thoughts and sharing interests. The percentage of the positive side among the Germans (82.6% and 68.8%) is higher than among the

Chinese (46.0% and 51.0%). To compare the four aspects within the groups, the percentage of understanding between the intimates and self disclosure with the intimates arranges number one and two in the German groups. The percentage of understanding between the intimates and sharing feelings with the intimates arranges number one and two in the Chinese groups.

Table 17: Self Disclosure with the Intimate

	German Religious	German non Religious	Chinese Religious	Chinese non Religious	General
Tell Thoughts	83.3	81.4	36.4	53.6	65.1
Hide Thoughts	13.6	7.0	25.0	16.1	15.3
Other	3.0	11.6	38.6	30.4	19.6

Missing Cases = 0

Table 18: Emotional Expression with the Intimates

	German Religious	German non Religious	Chinese Religious	Chinese non Religious	General
Express Feelings	78.8	69.8	70.5	76.8	74.6
Control Feelings	15.2	18.6	20.5	17.9	17.7
Other	6.1	11.6	9.1	5.4	7.7

Missing Cases = 0

What are the other answers? On the aspect of self disclosure with the intimates, the answers are: "Depends on the opposite side attitude, patient?", "Between your two given answers, not to tell too much not to hide too much", "Usually I

Table 19: Sharing Interests with the Intimates

	German Religious	German non Religious	Chinese Religious	Chinese non Religious	General
Share Interests	69.7	67.4	52.3	50.0	60.3
Have Own interests	13.6	14.0	36.4	42.9	26.3
Other	16.7	18.6	11.4	5.4	12.9

Missing Cases = 1

Table 20: Understanding between the Intimates

	German Religious	German non Religious	Chinese Religious	Chinese non Religious	General
Understand Much	90.0	86.0	77.3	82.1	84.7
Understand Less	3.0	2.3	20.5	12.5	9.1
Other	6.1	11.6	2.3	5.4	6.2

Missing Cases = 0

tell my private thoughts but I am upset", "Friends should trust each other without private thoughts to say", "Tell my private thoughts properly", "Tell my friend but not to tell my parents", "Keep back my thoughts properly". On the aspect of emotional expression with the intimates, the answers are: "Sometimes express while sometimes control", "Between your two given answers, both express and control", "Depends on what kind of feelings", "Usually I express. If upset, I control", "Sometimes it is hard to express my feelings", "Let it goes naturally", "I express more and control less". On the aspect of sharing interests with the intimates, the answers are: "Both sharing with her and also have my own", "Try to share with him as many as I can", "Some his interests I can share but some I can not", "I have mine while he has his but should have some common", "I have some difficulties to share". On the aspect of understanding each other, the answers are: "Try to understand her and keep my own beliefs at the same time", "Try to understand him but I am not sure if really", "Try to understand him and hope that he also understands me, "It is important to understand each other, not only one understands the other", "Always try to understand but not always succeed", "Sometimes try as much as I can, sometimes I need not that much", "Try to understand but not to force to do", "It cannot be friends without understanding".

5.2 Small Summary

To summarize the results: (1) Most people have intimate interactions with their partners or the intimates. Of course, intimate interactions are very detailed. Here is a rough description: to lay bare thoughts, to express feelings, to share interests, and to understand others. (2) People of the four groups have something similar on some aspects, and also have something different on some aspects. The differences are not reflected between the religious people and the non religious people but reflected between the German people and the Chinese people. Both the Germans and the Chinese pay attention mostly to understanding each other while the Germans put disclosure of thoughts on the second and the Chinese put the sharing feelings on the second. (3) The people who gave other answers are in small numbers. It seems that their answers have a common character which can be expressed by their own words "between one and two" and "It depends". That means their answers are between the two given answers one and two. If the two given answers are the two points of a scale, their answers are in a certain point between the two extreme points. It depends not only on what one side wants to do but also on what the other side's attitude and behaviour. It depends not only on what one wants to do but also on the consideration of the effect of doing it.

The questions are: (1) Since most people have intimate interactions with their partners or their intimates, the relationship between intimates should be in harmony. But in reality, the inharmonious phenomena between the intimates are common occurrence. How can this be explained? (2) There is a difference between the Germans and the Chinese on the aspects of self disclosure and sharing interests. Could this be attributed to a nature or a culture? (3) The other answers reflect a thought of appropriateness (a moderate course of action). Is it a skill of interaction or a philosophy of interaction? According to the investigation result, it is a skill from the view of the people. It can be also regarded as a principle of philosophy from the view of the research, the principle of "mean", not to go too far to control and not to go too near to reach the goal. The question is: In what situation do people behave as much as one likes heartily or enjoy oneself thoroughly?

5.3 Special Topic: Parents Bringing up Children

To investigate the interaction between the intimates, another two questions were raised in the questionnaire: "Why do parents bring up children? In order to have children remember them forever, or in order to ask children to provide for the aged, or in order to have the human beings multiply?" "Why do parents expect children to become useful persons? In order to bring honour to the family, or in order to make children to be independent, or in order to contribute to the society?" These two questions, in fact, are not to ask people about their interaction with children but to ask them about the relationship with children. Because the interaction between parents and children are quite different according to the age of parents-children and because the relationship between parents and children are complicated, not only according to the age of parents and children but also according to other factors, these general questions were raised.

In connection with the questions about "ancestors" and "descendants" in a previous section, these two questions again explore the relationship among humans and between humans and the divine. The differences between these two questions and the former two questions are: the former ones are more abstract, the latter ones are more concrete; the former ones are more general, the latter ones are more specific. These two questions want to ask people the purpose of bringing up children (for self, for children, for society, for the immortals, or for something else?) then proceed to explore their relationship. It is pity that the given answers of the two questions are not sufficient. But each of the questions allow people to give their own answers. It is supposed that people who have religious beliefs may associate having and bringing up children with immortals because they believe that it is God who gives life to everyone from the view of Christianity or they believe that everybody's life is predestined from the view of Buddhism (See Table 21 and 22).

The investigation results from Table 21 show that people who chose the given answers amounts to less than half and for each of the given answers only a small number of people chose. 64.1 % of the people gave their own answers. The investigation results from Table 22 show that people who agree that parents expect much of children for the sake of children's independence account for half and for the rest of the given answers only a small number of people chose. Some people gave their own answers. The differences between the people who have religious beliefs and the people who do not have religious beliefs from the two tables are not significant. The given answers did not have one which relate to the religious beliefs. It is important to see what are the other answers and the results from the interviews.

Why do parents bring up children? They can be categorized into several kinds. The answers are for self, for example, "Keep part of me alive in the children", "Have one who belongs to me", "Seek for love relationship with children", "Be

Table 21: Why Parents Bring up Children

	German Religious	German non Religious	Chinese Religious	Chinese non Religious	General
Remember Parents	21.2	7.0	6.8	10.7	12.4
Provide for the Aged	7.6	4.7	9.1	7.1	7.2
Humans Multiply	16.7	9.3	13.6	19.6	15.3
Other	53.0	76.7	70.5	62.5	64.1

Missing Cases = 2

Table 22: Why Parents Expect Children Much

	German Religious	German non Religious	Chinese Religious	Chinese non Religious	General
Honour Family	10.6	7.0	18.2	8.9	11.0
Children Independent	50.0	41.9	38.6	66.1	50.2
Continue Society	13.6	14.0	6.8	3.6	9.6
Other	25.8	37.2	36.4	21.4	29.2

Missing Cases = 0

happy to see children growing up", "Have a happy family life", "Experience having children to learn from it", "Make one's own life successful and meaningful; The answers are for society, for example, "Having children is the responsibility and duty of parents", "Be responsible for the future of the society", "It is a culture"; The answers are for God, for example, "It is fate", "Children are God's gift to us", "God is happy to see it"; The answers are that is natural, for example, "It is natural to be parents", "A sign of connection with the partner", "Child is a gift of love", "A natural process of human life"; Other answers which contain negative attitudes toward having children are, for example, "It is fault, an accident", "There are not rational reasons", "Cannot see any sense to have children". All those who gave their own explanations make up 54.1% of the total cases. Most of them think "for self" or "it is natural". Only 4 people had religious answers.

Why do parents expect much of Children? They can also be categorized into several kinds. The answers are for self, for example, "Make one's own sense of having done well", "Fulfil one's vanity", "Piece of oneself to the later world"; The answers are for children, for example, "Want children to have a successful life", "For children's healthy development", "Hope he will have good friends"; The answers are for God, for example, "Just for God", "It is God's decree"; The answers are for society, for example, "Be responsible for the future of world", "Fulfilling culture life"; Other answers are, for example, "I expect nothing", "They expect me", "It is natural and normal". All those who gave their own explanations make up 24.4% of the total cases. The explanations are not concentrated. Only 2 persons had religious answers.

The questions are: (1) The opinions on the question why do parents bring up children are so various that it is hard to get identical result. But if the answers are categorized into for self, for society, for the immortals, as part of nature, and others, the relatively high percentage is for self. It is 42.6%. While on the other question why do parents expect much of children, the relatively high rate is for children, it is 50.2%. Does it mean that giving birth to children and bringing up to children are separate concepts otherwise the two purposes should have certain connection? (2) The difference between the people who have religious beliefs and who do not have religious beliefs, nevertheless, was found in people's free answers but it amounts to a few people's answers. Does it mean that giving birth to children and bringing up of children has not much relationship with religious beliefs in the religious people's mind?

6. Dealing with Problems

Problems may appear in everyday life. They may appear in the interaction with strangers or with intimates. They may appear in any circumstances which are expected or unexpected. They check to one's progress or development. The serious problems are called setbacks. How do people deal with setbacks? In the questionnaire the questions are: "When you suffer setbacks in everyday life, do you usually find ways to solve them, or do you usually comfort yourself not to think about them, or do you usually pray?" "You may face many obstacles in everyday life, do most of them result from your own factors, or do most of them result from external factors, or are most of them decreed by fate?"

The process of dealing with problems is called problem solving. In psychology, there are two major forms of coping with stress. Stress is one kind of problems. The ways of problem solving in general may also be categorized into those two forms: One form is called problem focused. People can focus on the specific problem or situation that has arisen, trying to find some way of changing it or avoiding it in the future. Another form is called emotion focused. People can focus on alleviating the emotions associated with the problem situation, even if the situation itself cannot be changed (Atkinson, R.C. Atkinson, Smith, Bem and Hoeksema 1993: pp.602-606).

In reality, sometimes the problems are solved by the one or two ways but sometimes the problems are not solved. In psychology, something concerned with cognitive explanations of motivation and explanations why people succeed or fail in doing something is called attribution style. People usually attribute their successes or failures to four points: ability, effort, task difficulty, and chance. The four points can be divided into three dimensions: locus (internal and external), stability (stable and variable), and responsibility. The typical statement for internal stable attribution of success or failure is “I am clever or foolish”; for internal variable attribution of success or failure is “I am a hard worker or a lazy worker”; for external stable attribution of success or failure is “The task is easy or difficult”; for external variable attribution of success or failure is “I am lucky or unlucky” (Weiner 1980: pp.350-356).

These two questions in the questionnaire are aimed at testing people problem solving management and their attribution style. It is supposed that people who have religious beliefs may have a special mechanism to manage problems and have a special way to attribute problems besides the ways which other non religious people adopt, for example, they pray Jesus being a Christian or Buddha being a Buddhist. They believe that they can obtain comfort from God. They believe that God will give them advice and help them go from the darkness to the light. They attribute problems to fate. People who do not have religious beliefs may try to find other ways (here we do not make a value judgement temporarily on different ways) coping with problems (See Table 23 and 24).

6.1 Problem Solving

The investigation results from Table 23 show that most people are problem focused when they suffer setbacks. Only a small number of people are emotional focused, including those who usually pray when they suffer setbacks. Some people gave their own answers. Praying, from the perspective of the non religious people, is a kind of spiritual extrication from a predicament; from the perspective of the religious people, is a way to seek for help. Comparing the four groups, the percentage of people who are problem focused in the two religious groups is lower than the people in the two non religious groups. Though it amounts to more than half, the percentage of the non religious people is even higher. It is true that some religious people pray when they suffer setbacks but the percentage of those people is low, and the percentage of the non religious people on this point is even lower, almost zero.

What are the other answers? They can be simply categorized into two kinds, coping ways (try to cope with it) and natural ways (let it pass naturally). The examples of the coping ways are: "Problem focused plus emotion focused", "Problem focused plus pray", "Problem focused plus emotion focused plus pray". The examples of the natural way are: "Try to solve it, if it does not work, live with it", "Think about it and wait till it goes", "Accept it", "Live with it" or "Learn from it".

Table 23: How to Solve Problems

	German Religious	German non Religious	Chinese Religious	Chinese non Religious	General
Solve Problems	57.6	86.0	52.3	76.8	67.5
Comfort Oneself	6.1	4.7	2.3	16.1	7.7
Pray	10.6	0	25.0	1.8	9.1
Other	25.8	9.3	20.5	5.4	15.8

Missing Cases = 0

6.2 Attribution Style

The investigation results from Table 24 show that less than half of the people attribute obstacles to internal factors but it is the highest percentage among all the answers. A small number of people attribute obstacles to external factors or decreed by fate. Some people gave their own answers. Comparing the four groups, the percentage of people who attribute problems to internal factors in the German religious group is higher than the other three groups. Other differences are not significant.

What are the other answers? They can also be categorized into multiple factors and natural phenomena. The examples of multiple factors are: "Internal factors plus external factors", "Internal factors plus decreed by fate", "Internal factors plus external factors plus decreed by fate". The examples of natural phenomena are: "Obstacles are normal phenomena", "Most of them just happen without reasons", "Life itself brings them to me and they can help me growing up".

Table 24: How to Attribute Problems

	German Religious	German non Religious	Chinese Religious	Chinese non Religious	General
Internal Factors	54.5	30.2	36.4	33.9	40.2
External Factors	15.2	20.9	4.5	26.8	17.2
Decreed by Fate	3.0	2.3	13.6	8.9	6.7
Other	25.8	46.5	45.5	28.6	34.9

Missing Cases = 2

6.3 Small Summary

To summarize this section: (1) Most of people are problem focused when they suffer setbacks, especially those who are not religious. Those who define themselves as religious are also problem focused. In addition, some of them pray at the same time. A small number of religious people only pray when they suffer setbacks. (2) Many people attribute obstacles to internal factors. Some people attribute obstacles to external factors. Some people think that obstacles result from multiple factors. A small number of people think that obstacles are decreed by fate. Even they think so, they cannot rule out other possibilities. (3) A small number of people think that setbacks or obstacles are natural phenomena in life. Their attitude is "Just accept it and learn from it".

The questions are: (1) There are not many people who place hope on pray and attribute problems to fate. At least there are not many people who think that to pray is the only way to solve problems and fate is the only source of problems. Does it mean that the function of religious beliefs is not strong or has become weak? (2) Some people think that problems in life are natural and normal. Their attitude to problems is "just accept it and live with it". It seems that those people did not answer the questions "how" in the questionnaire directly. What are the differences between the sayings "pray for it" and "live with it"? What are the differences between the saying "it is fate" and "it is life"?

7. Immortals and People

The last two questions in the questionnaire are: "Sometimes when you do something, do you feel that your ancestors or god are watching you, or do you feel that other people are watching you, or do you feel both?", "When you do something, do you pay more attention to others' evaluation, or do you pay more attention to your own experience, or do you pay attention to both?". The aim is to ask people what they pay attention to when they do something, do they pay attention to themselves or do they pay attention to others? Then to ask people what kind of others they pay attention to, do they pay attention to the immortals or do they pay attention to the people? It is supposed that people who have religious beliefs and who do not have religious beliefs may feel differently when they do something, especially when they are in special situations.

In a Christian baptism ceremony, a young couple helped their one year old baby being baptized. At the end of the baptism, the priest asked the couple a question: What do you do as a couple if you have different opinions on bringing up the child? Whom do you listen to? The couple looked each other: "We discuss each other because this is a domestic affair (self experience)?" No. "We ask other friends because they may give you some advice and make a judgement (others' evaluation)?" No. The priest said: "You should ask God and listen to the God". The couple suddenly see the light. That is a priest's instruction. It means that as religious believers they can listen to God's teaching at any time. But as a non religious believer, one may ask: how can I know what God exactly says? It supposed that people who have religious beliefs may feel the presence of the immortals and pay attention to their decrees (See Table 25 and 26).

7.1 Who is Watching You

The investigation results from Table 25 show that sometimes when people do something they really feel as if they are being watched, by immortals, by people, or by both immortals and people. Comparing the four groups, there are more people in the two religious groups who feel either to be watched by the immortals or by both the immortals and people. There are more people in the two non religious groups who feel to be watched by people or to be watched by, they have their own answers, for example, by those who have very close relationship with them or by nobody at all. Their answers expressed a general meaning that they do not pay attention to who watch them. Instead, they answered: "Nobody watches me", "What I do has nothing to do with God and others", "I have a balance in my heart", "The conscience controls my behaviour", "I keep myself within the bounds of morals and values", "I see myself as if through a camera", "I just concentrate on the business or task itself", "I just do it and do it well".

Table 25: Who is Watching You

	German Religious	German non Religious	Chinese Religious	Chinese non Religious	General
Immortals	21.2	9.3	36.4	7.1	18.2
People	22.7	30.2	4.5	28.6	22.0
Both the above	34.8	11.6	40.9	25.0	28.7
Other	19.7	46.5	18.2	39.3	30.1

Missing Cases = 2

7.2 Whom You Pay Attention

The investigation results from Table 26 show that a small number of people only pay others' evaluations. More people pay attention to their own experience. Still more people not only pay attention to their own experience but also pay attention to others' evaluation when they do something. People who feel that they are watched by those who have close relationship with them pay attention to those "watchers" because they think that the watchers are important. Comparing the four groups, the difference between the religious people and the non religious people are not obvious. There are some differences between the German people and the Chinese people. On the aspect of paying attention to one's own experience, the Germans are a little more in number than the Chinese. On the aspect of paying attention to both self experience and others' evaluation, the Chinese are a little more in number than the Germans. A small number of people gave their own answers. Somebody mentioned God: "To see what I do conform to God's decree"; Somebody said: "It depends on what I do or am doing"; Other answers are: "Enjoy the process and the success", "Just do it then let it pass".

Table 26: What You Pay Attention

	German Religious	German non Religious	Chinese Religious	Chinese non Religious	General
Others' Evaluation	10.6	9.3	13.6	21.4	13.9
My Own Experience	37.9	32.6	22.7	17.9	28.2
Both the above	45.5	46.5	50.0	58.9	50.2
Other	4.5	11.6	13.6	1.8	7.2

Missing Cases = 1

7.3 Small Summary

A brief summary of the results from these two questions are: (1) Most people who have religious beliefs do feel the presence of the immortals, ancestors or god, when they do something sometimes though they may feel the existence of other people as well. Whereas, most people who do not have religious beliefs feel, instead of the immortals, the presence of other people or nobody at all when they do something. They concentrate on either task itself or their own conscience. (2) Most people pay attention to not only their own experience but also others' evaluation. Not many people only pay attention to one of the two aspects. The differences between the religious people and the non religious people are not obvious. There is a little difference between the German people and the Chinese people. There are more Germans than Chinese who pay more attention to one's own experience when they do something. (3) Those who gave their own answers on these two questions made the two questions connected. When they answered the first question "who is watching you?" they distinguished self, others, and task. It associates with the second question "whom you pay attention?" self, others, or both? Somebody mentioned here

“God”, which is just one of the answers in the first question. It means that God is watching them and they can pay attention to God.

The questions are: (1) Most religious people feel the presence of the immortals when they do something sometimes. If the immortals are regarded as the significant others, what is the interaction between the immortals and the people? (2) Combining the given answers and the answers from the research objects, what is the relationship among oneself, other people, the immortals, and the business?

Chapter 5: Results from Interview

The results from the interview are divided into several subjects as well. According to the design of the research, it is compatible with the results of the questionnaire. If the results from the questionnaire in the last chapter could give people a description of those who accepted the investigation, their beliefs and their interactions, the results from the interview in this chapter will give people an explanation of those who accepted the investigation, their beliefs and their interactions. Some questions which were raised in the last chapter could be answered in this chapter.

Just like Neuman's comparison between the quantitative analysis and qualitative analysis, the results from the interview are mainly in the form of words rather than in the form of numbers. Each of the subjects in this chapter contains a description of the results, a table of the contents in some sections, a comparison of the results, and questions which will be discussed in the next part. Some representative examples from the interview will be made in order to reveal the inner world of people and to have a better understanding of them. The table of contents in this chapter is different from the table of statistics in the last chapter. The table of statistics presents a result from the questionnaire in which everybody just gave one answer of each question. The table of contents presents a result from the interview in which many people gave multiple answers of each question. So the values in the table of contents are not the percentage of the cases but the numbers of person-time. The comparison of the results in this chapter is also different from the comparison of the results in the preceding chapter. The comparison of the results in the preceding chapter focused on the description (percentage) of the groups. The comparison of the results in this chapter focuses on the explanation (viewpoints) of the groups.

1. Personal Data

The general description of the people who accepted the interview is: There are 32 interviewees in total, 8 German religious persons, 9 German non religious persons, 8 Chinese religious persons, and 7 Chinese non religious persons. (See Table 27). Half of them are males and half of them are females. Their age is between 25 and 50, half of them under 35 years old and half of them over 36.

Table 27: Personal Data

	German Religious	German non Religious	Chinese Religious	Chinese non Religious	General
Male	5	5	4	2	16
Female	3	4	4	5	16
25-35	5	6	3	3	17
36-45	3	1	5	4	13
46-55	0	2	0	0	2
Single	7	7	1	1	16
Married	1	2	5	5	13
Divorced	0	0	2	1	3
No Uni Edu	0	1	2	1	4
Have Uni Edu	8	8	6	6	28
Study	3	2	2	1	8
Work	5	7	5	4	21
Home	0	0	1	2	3
Insufficient	1	0	3	2	6
Sufficient	8	6	5	5	24
Surplus	0	2	0	0	2
No Children	8	9	2	4	23
Have Children	0	0	6	3	9

Half of them are single and half of them are married including a few divorced. Most of them have no children while some of them have. Most of them have university education and only a few have not. Most of them work, some of them study, and a few are at home. Most of them think that their income is sufficient, some of them think that it is insufficient, a few think that it is surplus. The sample of the interview is not large. So the comparison of their personal data among the groups is omitted.

2. Beliefs in Death and Life after Death

The questions about beliefs in death and life after death in the interview are "What does it mean when your body is dead?", "Where will you go after your body is dead?", "Is a person's life eternal or limited?", "Is there a relationship between what one does now and in the hereafter?" The contents of those questions are similar to the questions in the questionnaire, only the forms are different. They are open questions without given answers, the interviewees may answer them freely. And each of the four questions has one word more than the questionnaire, which is "why". Someone may answer the questions in a certain way, why does he or she answer that way?

2.1 Beliefs in Death

The interview results about the beliefs in death can be categorized into five kinds. The first is to believe that body is dead but soul or mind will continue living in another place and in another form. It is clear that people believe in not only the continuity of life after death but also who continue the life (the soul or mind) and how the life continues (another place and another form). The second is to believe that life will continue after death but they do not know how it continues. It means that people believe in the continuity of life after death but the picture of how it continues is vague. The third is to believe that a person's body is dead and everything of the person is finished. It is clear that people believe that everything will pass away along with the death of a body. The fourth is to believe that life will finish after death but they still hope on its continuity. Or to believe that life will continue after death but they still fear death. It means that people believe that death of a body is or is not the end of life but they do not want to face it squarely. The fifth is to say that they do not know what will be after death because they are still alive and have not that experience yet. What does it mean? Do they believe that they will know everything when they die? Or do they have not any belief about death and life after death? (See Table 28 and 29)

Table 28: Meaning of Body Death

	German Religious	German non Religious	Chinese Religious	Chinese non Religious	Total
Soul Continue	3	0	4	0	7
How Continue	3	0	0	0	3
Life Finish	2	8	2	7	19
Hope to Live	1	2	1	1	5
Do not Know	0	1	2	0	3

Table 29: Place to Go after Death

	German Religious	German non Religious	Chinese Religious	Chinese non Religious	Total
Another Place	6	0	3	0	9
Here or There	1	0	2	0	3
Sleep in Soil	1	5	0	3	9
Fear Death	0	1	0	0	1
Not Be Sure	0	4	3	4	11

To compare the viewpoints of the four groups, the examples of all the five viewpoints can be found in the religious groups. Besides the belief that the death of a body is not the end of life is supposed as the representative perspective of the religious people, the belief that the death of a body is the end of life is also expressed by a few people in these two groups. For example: "My life is gone when my body is dead", "Nothing else will happen after I die", "A death of a man just likes a lamp die out". These expressions show no differences from the expressions of the people in the two non religious groups. The examples of the viewpoints that life will continue after the death of a body were not found in the two non religious groups. People in these two groups believe that when the body is dead then everything of the person is finished. As to the question of they go after death, the examples of the expression going to another place or not to know where to go can be found in the two religious groups. The examples of the expression sleeping in soil or not to know where to go can be found in the two non religious groups (See Example 1-8).

Example 1: This is an example of those who believe that body is dead but soul or mind will continue living in another place and in another form. "I believe that only my body is dead but my mind and soul will survive. There are many reports about it. I think that it is true. There are some people whose body is physically dead, whose brain does not function anymore, they are dead. Then their soul left the body like a bird and is able to recognize what is going on. I think that the stories are convincing. I believe that my body will die but my mind and soul will live in another dimension and in another atmosphere. Then there will be a reincarnation. My mind will go into a new material body. My soul will come back with a different appearance into that body. Though my brain is physically dead, my mind and soul is not a physical thing, it is spiritual."

"I want to believe it because it will be unsatisfying if there is only one life. It is too short. Everything which belongs to me will be gone along with the death of my body. So the religious notion is pleasant for me. It gives me consolation. I would not say that I will go to the heaven after death. I think that maybe I am still on this planet but in another dimension. We cannot look into those dimensions. There are several stages. The highest dimension is near to the earth, while the lower dimension is far from the living beings. The ghosts will go to the lower dimension. I hope that I can go to a higher one. One day, I will reincarnate. It will not be the same person but there will be a connection between me with the next one."

Example 2: This is another example of those who believe that body is dead but soul or mind will continue living in another place and in another form. "Death means that I myself with the soul get rid of my body. I will go to a different place, find a different body. It is just the same as a person, who takes off his dress before he goes to bed, and then takes a new dress again when he gets up the next morning. It is also the same as a person who drives a car. When the car is broken, he will get rid of it and change to a new one. The dress and the car are just like the body. You get rid of one body and get another one. You get rid of the old car and change to a new one"

"Life after death for me, I cannot tell from experience because I do not know. I can only talk about what I hear and what I read. It makes a lot of sense to me. It is due to the law of karma. My action in this life and previous life, especially the action in this life determines my next life. For example, if I live with this body in this life very cruelly, I hurt other people, my behaviour is not really like a human being but an animal, I may take a body of an animal next life. If I live with this body in this life very morally, I have human values, I help people and love people, I will naturally get a body of the humans. You can make progress in this moral development."

Example 3: This is an example of those who believe that life will continue after death but do not know how it continues. "A death of a physical body, from the typical view of science, life is finished. From the people's belief, I say that life will continue in another way. I cannot explain what kind of way the life will be. I am a person, my body is gone, the body cannot be without a soul, and the soul cannot be without a body. From the religious belief, I cannot say that the life is finished forever but I cannot imagine how it continues. So I believe that there is an eternal life but I cannot say how."

"I do not know where I will go after death. The dead person is me. It finished. It will be a totally different kind of being. I cannot think about it because our thinking is absolutely connected with the earth, with life. I can only see or imagine in this world. It will not be another person, it is me, depending on my definition. But I would say, yes, in another way."

Example 4: This is another example of those who believe that life will continue after death but do not know how it continues. "Oh, when my body is dead, you mean the end of life? (Ask: what do you think?) Do you mean how it goes on? I think somehow it goes on. I cannot say how but it is not to immigrate into another person. It goes on in some kind. (Ask: can you describe it?) No. But I believe that it goes on. It will not be in this world but in some other space and other time. (Ask: can you describe it?) No. I do not have exact imaginations. I do not think that I will have contact with this place anymore."

Example 5: This is an example of those who believe that body is dead then everything will finish along with the death of the body. "I think that everything is finished if my body is dead. I don't believe that I will have other opportunities after death. I will loose my body and head after death. How can a person think without head? I will no longer have my personality after death. The energy of my body will return to the earth. If I believed that there would be a life after death, which is what I am cheating myself. I just have this one life. If there are really opportunities for me after death, OK, I will accept it. But I do not believe it. I cannot cheat myself because nobody knows the life after death."

Example 6: This is another example of those who believe that body is dead then everything will finish along with the death of the body. "A person will not exist anymore after his body is dead, return to the nature. Everybody experiences birth and death. It is a natural process. To imagine how many people there will be on earth if everybody lives 500 years? I hope that I could live that long, long till forever. But it is not meaningful. It cannot comfort me. I cannot place hope in this life on the next life. If everybody has that kind of hope, what hope of the society would have in the future? I will go to the earth, return to the nature. Maybe the elements of my body can compose other lives, that elements are fertilizer. I would rather be fertilizer than something else polluting environment."

Example 7: This is an example of those who believe that life will finish after the death of a body but still place hope on its continuity. "I do not believe in anything which will happen after death but I hope that it happens. I don't want to die, I want to live. I am not sure about the future. It is interesting to think about life after death. There are a lot of theses about it. I fear that there will be nowhere to go after death. Religion, it would not help me because I do not see the reason to believe in it. Perhaps my spirit or my soul is different. What is operating now is thinking. That is my consciousness. That will be gone after my body is dead. Then I will not have anything anymore."

Example 8: This is an example of those who believe that life will continue after the death of a body but still fear death. "The belief and the real experience are two different matters. For example, I believe in samsara. That is the knowledge which I obtained from books. That is not the experience of my own. If there is a person who got an incurable disease, you can comfort him very clearly and logically. If I myself got that disease, I cannot be that comfortable. From the knowledge of samsara, the death of a body is just like an old organ, useless. If let me imagine my death, I cannot be that flexible. I must be afraid of that."

"It is hard to say where I will go after death. It depends on what I did previously and what I think before I die. According to my performance, I may not go to a good place. This is the effect of "ye" (action). Ye will drive me to a certain place. Ye can guide me to experience something in my life. If I can observe the rules in which I believe, I can be a man next life. If I cannot do that good, I will go to a bad road. If I believe in it sincerely, I will make effort to reach the realm of good."

The above examples not only described what people believe in detail but also explained why they believe that in varying degrees. Those who believe that there will be a life after death described how their spirit leaves their physical body and continues living. It likes a bird throwing on new plumage flying to another world starting a new life. It likes a person changing a new clothes setting foot on a new journey. People believe it because they heard or read something about those stories and think that they are convincing. It is knowledge which is acquired by them. It is an outlook which is internalized by them. It makes them feel satisfied with life. Those who believe that the death of a body is the end of life stated their reasons. The brain is the material of thinking. Man cannot think anything if the brain is not functioning. It is impossible that a man is living with a dead brain. They described their life after death: return to the earth (be buried, the tradition way in people's mind) as fertilizer.

Believing or not believing that there is a life after death are the two completely different point of views. Death itself is a serious topic. No matter what a person believes, nobody wants to die and nobody can avoid death. That is why some people believe that there is a life after death but still fear death; Some people believe that the death of a body is the end life but still hope to live long. The question is: Is there a gap between beliefs and experience? In addition, some people said clearly that the death of a body is the end of life from the view of science, while life will continue after the death of a body from their beliefs. The question is: Can these two contradictory views cooperate in one person's mind?

2.2 Life after Death

The interview results about life after death can be categorized into three kinds. The first is to believe that life is eternal because the soul will exist after the death of a body, the spirit will go somewhere else, the mind is never born and will never die. There is a relationship between what one does now and one will in the hereafter because God will make a judgement for each person after they die which determines their life in the future, what they do in this life will have consequences in the next life. The second is to believe that life is limited because modern science tells people that as soon as the body dies nothing else of the person will be alive, when the body dies then everything is finished. There is no relationship between what one does now and hereafter because a dead person cannot think anything anymore and cannot do anything anymore and will not know anything anymore. However some people who hold this belief said that life is limited but the meaning of life is infinite. There is a saying which some people repeated when they talked about life after death: good will be rewarded with good and evil with evil. The third is to say: I hope that life is eternal but do not know. I think about it but do not believe anything. I seldom think about it, a distant future. (See Table 30 and 31)

Table 30: Life Eternal or Life Limited

	German Religious	German non Religious	Chinese Religious	Chinese non Religious	Total
Life Eternal	6	0	4	0	10
Life Limited	1	6	4	7	18
Do not Know	1	3	0	0	4

Table 31: This Life and Next Life

	German Religious	German non Religious	Chinese Religious	Chinese non Religious	Total
Has Relationship	6	0	5	0	11
No Relationship	1	6	1	7	15
Do not Know	1	3	2	0	6

To compare the viewpoints of the four groups, the examples of both the two opposite perspectives can be found in the two religious groups. The belief that life is eternal is supposed as the representative perspective of the religious people. While the belief that life is limited is supposed as the representative perspective of the non religious people. But the non religious concept is also expressed by a few people in the two religious groups. They said: "Everybody will die at a certain age", "Nobody can live forever only others may remember him", "Life is nothing but someone lives longer and someone lives shorter". These expressions are the same as the expressions of the people in the two non religious groups. The examples of the perspective that life is eternal were not found in the two non religious groups. They believe that life is limited. As to the question if there is retribution after death, the examples of believing in retribution after death or not knowing if there is retribution after death can be found in the two religious groups. The examples of not believing retribution after death or not to know if there is retribution or not can be found in the two non religious groups (See Example 9-14).

Example 9: This is an example of those who believe that life is eternal. "Life is eternal because I believe in God and believe that man is created by God. It is God who placed his spirit in man's heart. He used mud moulding man's body. Because there is a God's spirit in man's body, man can present their vivid lifelike. The life of the body is limited while the spirit is eternal. Because God created man, God has requirements to man, that is what man can do and cannot do. God will make a judgement for man's behaviour. Those whose behaviour conform to the God's requirements can go to heaven. Those whose behaviour is regarded as bad according to the God's judgement will go to hell. What one does in his or her lifetime in this world will influence his or her future."

Example 10: This is another example of those who believe that life is eternal. "The definition of life in the religion in which I believe can be explained as: there is an eternal unchangeable I. In some other religion the eternal and unchangeable I can be called soul. It means that there is a living material which can leave the man's body continue living without beginning without end. The purpose of the religion is to direct a way for people to reveal the world in its true colour. That is to extricate oneself from the suffering in this world (samsara) to reach the realm of eternal happiness (nirvana). It is not easy to reach that realm, very few people can, it can be counted on one's finger, Buddha is a good example. People strive for that from one level to another. Of course, there is a relationship between one does now and hereafter. If one does not make effort today, he will be always suffering. All false appearance in this world is real for him. For example, if I work hard, I may get closer and closer to Buddha. If I am lazy, I may become an animal in the hereafter. How can an animal's life be compared with a life of man?"

Example 11: This is an example of those who believe that life is limited. "Life is limited but the meaning of life is eternal. A person's life ends on the day his body is dead. All those so called spirits or souls cannot exist without a material substance. It is difficult to talk clearly about the spiritual things. Many abstract matters are good, propel human beings forward, humans intelligence developed. But life cannot exist alone apart from material substance. There is no relationship between what one does now and hereafter but there is a relationship between what one does now and the future before he or she dies. If you often make a risk choice, you may die quickly. If you do not, you may die slowly. This is the relationship."

Example 12: This is another example of those who believe that life is limited. "My life is limited. I can only live until my body is dead. Maybe there is another life continuing in another world afterwards. (Ask: what do you think?) My parents told me that I will go to heaven after I die. There will be someone who takes me there. I will see clouds and angels there. I want to wait and see if the angels are going to accompany me. I think that what you believe depends on what your parents tell you. If your parents tell you that you will be a dead person when your body is dead, then you will believe it. There is no relationship between what one does now and hereafter. If I did something wrong in this life, for example, I hurt somebody, some people may say that you will deserve punishment next life. I would say: no, there is not a relationship."

Example 13: This is an example of one who thinks a lot about what will be after his body is dead but does not believe anything. "I do not know if life is eternal or limited. I can think about it but I have not any reason to choose anything for being the right one. There is no hint to choose what is right and what is wrong at the moment. I just have to choose that I do not want to die. (Ask: What do you believe?) Nothing. I tried not to believe anything. My personal experience tells me that I usually make life very uncomfortable if I believe in something. The believers themselves may not really believe but they get others to believe. I prefer thinking but not to believe anything. I am not sure but thinking is interesting. I do not know if there is a relationship between what one does now and hereafter. I do not want to die. I can think a lot about it but I cannot choose."

Example 14: This is an example of one who seldom think about what will be after his body is dead, a distant future. "Life should be limited. One can live until one's body is dead. This is a view from natural science. As to the relationship between what one does now and hereafter, I seldom think about it, I do not want to think about it as well. It is a matter of a distant future, to think about it, is not realistic. I think that doing good things will deserve good and doing bad things will deserve bad. One may not certainly go to heaven or hell. Maybe one will get repay just this life in this world. This is so called heaven and hell. If you are happy, you are in the heaven; If you are suffering, you are in the hell. That is the heaven and hell in the man's world."

From the examples, it is not difficult to find why there are some people who did not choose the given answers in the questionnaire but gave their own answers. The questions like where will you go or what will you do after death are too concrete to answer. People may believe that everything stops after death but they may not definitely know where to go, for example, to go to the graveyard. There are other funeral forms except the graveyard. The expression of "to go to the graveyard" in the questionnaire refers to being buried tactfully. Some people may understand this expression differently and said: "nowhere to go". Some people said: "do not know where". People may believe that life will continue after death but they may not know exactly what to do, for example, to do something like now. The expression "to do what he wants in this life" in the questionnaire means a spiritual sustenance. It might be too concrete to think and to know. Many people said that they do not know what they will do or they stressed to do well in this life. To compare the results from the questionnaire and the results from the interview, it shows that the same answers in the questionnaire do not definitely imply the same meaning. For example, both religious people and non religious people say if one cannot do what he wants in this life, he will not have the opportunities later. The religious people mean that they cannot do this but may do that in the hereafter. The non religious people mean that they cannot do anything anymore.

Those examples show that belief is the feeling that something in people's mind is regarded as real and true (a definition of belief in dictionaries). Religious belief is something in the beyond which is accepted by people as real and true. In this section, something in the beyond refers to the concept of death and life after death of individuals. It is a general abstract view rather than a specific concrete view. For religious believers, it is easy to answer the questions generally but it is not easy to answer the questions specifically. If they did not choose a given answer which they think too specific and concrete to answer, it does not certainly mean that their own answers are different from the given answers in general.

2.3 Small Summary

To summarize the people's beliefs in death and life after death from those whose self given identities are religious: (1) A human beings' body will physically die finally but the spiritual part, soul or mind, will continue living. (2) The spiritual part will go to another place and live in another form. (3) What will they do? This is a question which few people can answer in detail though some people can imagine the life there. (4) Good will be rewarded with good and evil with evil. This is a law not only in the next world but also in this world. A few people whose self given identities are religious but their beliefs are not identical with other religious people, conversely, their beliefs showed no differences from the people whose self identity are non religious.

To summarize the people's beliefs in death and life after death from those whose self given identities are non religious: (5) Everything will be finished along with the death of a body. What is called soul or mind cannot exist without a functioning brain. (6) They will disappear in this world after they die. They may return to the earth as fertilizer of other living things. (7) They cannot do anything anymore after they die. What is important is to do everything thing well in this world. (8) Good will be rewarded with good and evil with evil. This is a law in this world. Good ones will be praised and bad ones will be cursed by later generations.

3. Relationship between the Living and the Dead

The questions about the relationship between the living and the dead in the interview are: "What do you think about your dead relatives, are they still living somewhere or did they disappear forever?" "Is it a reality or a fantasy if your dead relatives appear in front of you?" "Our ancestors or God gave us life, do they have power to dominate us in this world?" "Our descendants will live in this world after we leave here, what is the meaning of that?" These four questions are also similar to those in the questionnaire. Each of them add one word again more than the questionnaire, which is "why".

3.1 Relationship with Dead Relatives

The interview results about the dead relatives can be categorized into three kinds. The first is to believe that their dead relatives are still living somewhere because their soul is somewhere. God made a judgement for them and sent them to heaven or hell. People may meet their dead relatives after they themselves die. Though few of them have the experience that their dead relatives appearing in front of them, most of them believe that it is a reality if they do appear. The ghosts cannot be seen with human eyes but people can experience it with their heart. The second is to believe that their dead relatives died just like they themselves will die. The dead will never exist again in reality. They can only exist in people's memory. Though many people have had the experience of losing relatives, few of them have had the experience of the dead relatives appearing in front of them. They may appear in dreams but it is a fantasy. It is because that they miss them so much that it seems that they appear. The third is to say: I do not know or I am not clear about it because I have not such experience and it cannot be proved (See Table 32 and 33).

Table 32: Think about Dead Relatives

	German Religious	German non Religious	Chinese Religious	Chinese non Religious	Total
Still Living	6	0	6	1	13
Die forever	2	9	1	5	17
Do not know	0	0	1	1	2

Table 33: Contact with Dead Relatives

	German Religious	German non Religious	Chinese Religious	Chinese non Religious	Total
Reality	1	0	2	0	3
Fantasy	6	7	5	6	24
Not Clear	1	2	1	1	5

To compare the viewpoints of the four groups, the examples of all the three perspectives can be found in the two religious groups. Besides the belief that their dead relatives are still living somewhere because their soul continues is supposed as the representative perspective of the religious people. The belief that their dead relatives died forever is also expressed by a few people in the two religious groups. For example: "They died and they only live in the memory of me and the memory of God. I cannot contact them in the way to see them, to hear them, to talk to them, but I can look back their life when they were alive." This paragraph has something similar to those expressed by the people in the two non religious groups because it contains the meaning of "died". But the phrase "in the memory of God" is not the representative expression of the non religious people because God never exists from their point of view.

The examples of the belief that the dead relatives died just like they themselves will die is the representative perspective in the two non religious groups. Only very few people in these two groups believe that their dead relatives are still living somewhere. For example: "I visited my dead father at his tomb. I felt that he was just by my side looking at me. (Ask: do you think that it is a reality or a fantasy?) I do not know. I talked to him. I thought that he heard. (Ask: did he say something to you?) No. While, when I die, I believe that I will disappear from the world. My father is different from me." This paragraph of words showed another contradictory thought: "my father is still somewhere" but "I will disappear" (See Example 15-20)

Example 15: This is an example of those who believe that their dead relatives are still living somewhere. "My dead relatives, just like me in the future, were judged by God, then went to heaven or hell. (Ask: if you can go to heaven, and your dead relatives are there, will you meet each other?) Yes, of course. We will see each other there. I have not the experience that my dead relatives came to me.

But I saw them in my dreams. This is what I said, I believe that the soul lives forever. It does not exist in the material world but it can appear in front of you in an invisible form. It depends on what you believe. Experiencing if your dead relatives appearing in front of you is just like believing if there is a God in the world. If you believe it, it is there. Nobody can show us God, you experience God with your heart."

Example 16: This is another example of those who believe that their dead relatives are still living somewhere. "The dead relatives in my family went to the place where they wanted to go. (Ask: where are the places they go?) For example, paradise. My grandmother is there, I know that. (Ask: can you contact her?) Not yet because I have not reached that level. If I am peaceful and quiet in heart, I can. Our relationship changed after she left this world. We do no longer have the relationship of grandmother and granddaughter. But I respect her very much because she is my ancestor. (Ask: do you have the experience of meet with her?) No, not yet. But I know this circumstance. (Ask: is it a reality?) Yes, it is a reality. It is not the reality which we can see with our eyes. For example, ghost, we cannot see it but it exists."

Example 17: This is an example of those who feel that their dead relatives are still living somewhere and they want to believe it. "If a person died very young, I feel that he did not die, he is still there. My former husband died because of disease. I buried him a few months ago. He died, I am sad, he is too young to die. I feel that he is still there. This is my own experience. We divorced but we are still friends. We are young after all. He drank a lot when he was alive, just knew pleasure seeking. It is better to work hard, one can live longer. Life is decreed by fate. For example, you are rich, but you spent all of your money when you were young, then you will not have money left. You are poor now, but your future is bright if you make effort. (Ask: do you have experience of meeting with him?) No. But it seems that he still lives there, in that big city."

Example 18: This is an example of those who believe that their dead relatives disappeared in this world forever. "Someone died, it makes a great impact on the people who are living. You can feel that you think of them all the time. This is memory. Everybody will become old and die. To do as much as you can when you are alive, to live well and meaningfully is important. You ask that it is a reality or a fantasy if my dead relatives appear in front of me, I say that it is a fantasy. Everybody may have this fantasy. All kinds of fantasies may appear if one thinks too much. It is a normal phenomenon."

Example 19: This is another example of those who believe that their dead relatives disappeared in this world forever. "Those who died will not appear again. If you treat others well when they are alive, to give them a little more help, go accompany them, you will feel at ease and justified when they die. Almost every time when I visited my grandparents, I see them becoming older a little bit. They are in their 90's already. I cannot find a good way to help them and feel upset in heart. What I can do is to give them money and buy something to eat for them. I have not the experience that my dead relatives appear in front of me because my close relatives are still alive. My grandfather on my father side died but I did not that special experience because I had few contact with him when he was alive. Only those who are close to you and important to you, who died, you will have that experience."

Example 20: This is an example of those who think that their dead relatives can be only alive in their memory. "I have a lot of dead relatives. They are in my memory. Several people whom I know died already. I remember them. That is the way they are still alive. I can remember what they did and what they said when they were alive. I can think what they would say if they were alive. I just imagine that they can contact with me. If I die and if nobody else remembers them anymore, they are gone. It is a fantasy if someone said that their dead relative really appear in front of them. That is imagination. But there might be not much difference between reality and fantasy. I do not want to make a clear distinction."

These examples make a further explanation why some people believe that their dead relatives are still living somewhere and why their dead relatives disappeared in the world forever. Is it a reality or a fantasy if the dead relatives appear? Fantasy, most people said. Even some people believe that their dead relatives are still living somewhere and they can contact them in a certain way, they hardly believe that their dead relatives can return to the man's world. It is interesting to see how people express their religious beliefs. For example: "Experiencing if your dead relatives appear in front of you is just like believing if there is a god in the world. Nobody can show you a god, you experience God with heart"; "I have not the experience of meeting with my dead relatives because I have not reached that level. If I am peaceful and quiet in heart, I may meet with them". What do these expressions mean? It means that the interaction between the living people and the dead people can only occur when the heart of the living people is there.

3.2 Relationship with Ancestors and God

The interview results about the relationship between people who are living in this world and their ancestors can be categorized into four kinds. The first is to believe that ancestors or God (depending on people's beliefs) have power. In the preceding chapter, we discussed the same issue. It pointed out that ancestors are different from God. Ancestors did live in this world and ancestors were created by God. But if people believe that regardless ancestors or God are the immortals in the beyond and worship them, there will be no difference. When people talked about it, they used different terms according to their own religious beliefs. They use the word “influence” rather than “dominate” to describe the immortals. They believe that ancestors or God have power to influence them on the one hand and also believe that ancestors or god give them freedom on the other hand. The second is to believe that ancestors or God have no power over humans because ancestors died and God never exists in the world. If people say that ancestors have power, it is because of what they did in the past. If people say that God has power, it is because that people created it in their mind. The third is half-believing and half-doubting. Some people do not believe completely that ancestors or God have power but they think that it is efficacious sometimes if they pray them for help. Some people doubt a lot that ancestors or God have power but they are afraid to speak out, at least they think it is better not to speak ill of them. The fourth is to say: I do not know. I do not want to believe anything (See Table 34).

Table 34: Relationship with Ancestors and God

	German Religious	German non Religious	Chinese Religious	Chinese non Religious	Total
Have Power	5	0	6	0	11
No Power	3	8	0	6	17
Half-Believing	0	0	1	1	2
Do not Know	0	1	1	0	2

To compare the viewpoints of the four groups, the examples of all the four perspectives can be found in the two religious groups. The belief that ancestors or God have power over humans is supposed as the representative perspective of the religious people. However, many religious people entrusted this supernatural power only to God and they attribute heritage or cultural creativities to ancestors. When people answered the questions, they chose the words between God and ancestors according to their beliefs. If they believe in God, they would say that God has the power. If they worship the ancestors, they would say that ancestors have the influence. If they believe in Karma, they would say previous life has power to influence future life. The examples of the belief that ancestors or God has no power are the common perspective of the people in the two non religious groups (See Example 21-26).

Example 21: This is an example of those who believe in the immortal's power. Those immortals are spiritual beings. "My ancestors influence me by their heritage. But I have my own free will at the same time. Their opinions influence me, what they may think can come to my mind, but I can make my own choice. My grandmother died. I know her personally. I know what she thought and what she told me. My mother had the experience that her dead father really appeared to her directly. I do not believe in God but I believe that there are some spiritual beings, for example angels, though I have not ever seen her. (Ask: do you think that the spiritual beings participate in your decision making?) Ya, maybe. If I get upset or angry, it may result from some demons."

Example 22: This is another example of those who believe in the immortal's power. This immortal is God. "This is not from my experience but my belief. I believe that God does not interfere with us so much in our life. He gives us free will. We separate from God at one point, and this separation makes us suffering in this world. It was our own decision. At another point, we have desire to ask: May this life make sense to me in the way I am living? For example, being a rich man or becoming popular, does it make sense to me? No, no sense to me anymore, I think. So we look for some other values. At this moment, we ask some questions about the purposes of life. Then it might be that God interferes us. He will tell us: you are struggling in your mind, now it is the time to change your thoughts. I try to ask myself what is the cause of suffering? Then God gives me the answer: to go to the books, to go to the people. Somehow they come to my life and answer my questions. Because of this, everything can suddenly make sense. In this way, God interfere us. Usually he keeps distance from us and gives us freedom. We can do what we want. Once we have questions to ask him, he will react."

Example 23: This is an example of those who believe that the immortals cannot have power over the humans. "Children are very much determined by their parents because the parents influence them. But the parents cannot really influence the children's life after they die. The influences of the parents are only from the past. It does not matter if your parents are living or dead, you can have a different attitude towards your parents because you are an independent person."

Example 24: This is another example of those who believe that the immortals cannot have power over the humans. "In fact, the ancestors or God has no power over us. But if you believe that your ancestors are still alive in a paradise, or if you believe in God, it will have influence. This influence is nothing but something you created. It is not true. I do not believe in God, he will not influence me. The ancestors died already, how could they involve in our affair?"

Example 25: This is an example of those who half-believing that the immortals have power over the humans. "I think that my ancestors may give us energy. My mother always burn paper money in the New Year's Eve for my dead grandparents saying: please give us energy, bless my daughter study well. She also burn joss sticks for the Buddha saying: bless our whole family is well, bless my daughter have a pleasant journey from China to Germany. In order to celebrate Guanyin Buddha's birthday, she abstained from eating meat. She believes it sincerely. I do not believe that much but a little. My elder sister and her husband do business. In order to make a deal successfully, they went to a big temple far away from home to pray especially. It was really efficacious. I think that it is because of both their effort and God's help. My mother often told me: if you want to prostrate yourself before the Buddha, you can only think of him not of others. If you think of others, it will not work. She does it very earnestly. I cannot do it like her."

Example 26: This is another example of those who half-doubting that the immortals have power over the humans. "I do not think that I believe the immortals having power over the humans but I am afraid to speak it out. If I speak it out to those who believe in the immortals' power, they will be angry. If the immortals really have that power and they hear what I said, I ask for trouble. Though I do not believe it, I still observe some of the customs. I would rather say that they have the power than say that they do not have. You have better not to offend them, at least not to speak ill of them. Otherwise, they may punish you."

These examples illustrate the role of the ancestors or God in people's mind. This role cannot be described in general. It can only be described in a certain relationship. In the relationship between God and the people who sincerely believe in it, the role of God is a charismatic one. It is just like Max Weber studied, this is one of the three types of domination (the other two types are traditional one and rational one). People respect God and want to get close to God. In the relationship between God and people who half believe in it, the role of God is one whom people feel a bit doubt and a bit fear, and want to keep distance from. Of course, there is not a relationship between God and people who do not believe in it. It can be seen from the interview that ancestors and

God, though both are immortals in the people's mind, God is regarded as a charismatic supernatural being, ancestors are not given the nature of God by most people. However, ancestor worship, like the example 25 described, maybe still popular in China, especially in the rural areas. But it is not as representative as it is supposed in this research. It is because of the influences of the western religion, some of the Chinese in Germany may regard going to church as a fashion rather than kowtow before the ancestors' statue.

3.3 Relationship with Descendants

The interview results about the relationship between the people who are living in this world and their descendants can be categorized into four kinds. These four kinds are not divided according to the answers but according to the starting point from which people proceed. The first is to proceed from the descendants. For example: I can only leave over some material things to my descendants. I educate them when I am alive. I pass my gene to them. The second is to proceed from the people themselves. For example: My descendants are the extension of my life. They are the extension of my family. The third is to proceed from the descendants and themselves. For example: I want to develop a loving relationship with my descendants. If I help them now then they may help me but I am not sure. The fourth is to stress individual independence. For example: My descendants have their own life. They are other human beings. When my life is finished, I will not know anything anymore. Reproduction is a natural process of the humans (See Table 35).

To compare the viewpoints of the four groups, the examples of all the four perspectives can be found in each group. The thought that everybody is an independent individual is the representative opinion in each group except in the Chinese Religious group. The influence of older generation to younger generation can only emerge when the older people are alive. Of course, this influence may continue even when the older people die. The influence of the younger generation to the older generation can only exist when the older people are alive. This influence will have no function when the older people die. The examples of other perspectives are dispersed in some groups. It seems that the generational relationship is closer among the Chinese than among the Germans. It is not only reflected from the questionnaire but also reflected from the interview. The Chinese people from the investigation show that they more or less place their own hope rather than the children's hope to the children. The concept of "extension of my life" or "successor of my cause", and so on, expressed a spiritual sustenance of the Chinese (See Example 27-30).

Table 35: Relationship with Descendants

	German Religious	German non Religious	Chinese Religious	Chinese non Religious	Total
For Descendant	2	3	1	0	6
For Self	1	1	3	1	6
Mutual Benefit	1	1	3	1	6
Independence	5	6	1	5	17

Example 27: This is an example of those who think that they can give something to the descendants. "The relationship between I and my descendants is similar to the relationship between my ancestors and I. I can help my children something. It is not in the way that I prevent them doing something or I help them doing something. It is in the way that I educate them as much as I can. It means that I educate them by the way of what I do for them. In the process of bringing them up, they learned from me, they may adapt it, they may continue it."

Example 28: This is an example of those who think that they can feel a certain self satisfaction from their descendants. "My descendants are the extension of my life because they and I have the same kind of blood. Descendants, for the humans, are the extension of the mankind; for the individuals, are the extension of family. It is a natural law to pass on life from generation to generation. If woman do not want to give birth to children, the whole population will be decreased. It also means that my gene will exit. If I have descendants, I am their parents, this relationship will exist forever. The communication between the living and the dead is not that we normally talk to each other but that we contact with our soul."

Example 29: This is an example of those who think that the relationship between the descendants and they themselves are mutual benefit. "There are some connections with each other. I would like my children understand something. I think that it is important for the human life to develop positive loving relationships, the relationships with people and the relationship with God. It will lead to happiness. I hope my children will help people, to be helpful for the society, for the mankind. It is what I want and what my children will do. If you love others, others will love you. If you help others often, others will help you when you need."

Example 30: This is an example of those who think that the relationship between the descendants and they themselves are relatively independent. "Giving birth to children and educating them are the duties of parents. We will die after they grow up. Then the children again observe the same way of their parents. This is a law which you must obey no matter you go to heaven or to hell. I don't think that my children are the extension of my life. Some people said that the children only belong to them because they think that they gave the life to children. In fact, it is God who gives the life of children."

These examples illustrate that the role of descendants in the interview cannot be described in general as well. Some people think that God created man, including themselves and their children. So they are equal before God. Each of them is an independent individual. In this sense, everybody has a relationship with God but may not have a certain relationship with each other. Because God gives a soul to everybody, even if the body of somebody dies, they can still contact each other, for example, their ancestor or their descendants. Only the form of the contact will be different. Some people think that it is not God but parents give birth to children. Parents are the root of children. So they have permanent relationship with each other, with their ancestors and their descendants. Because human life is limited, they can no longer keep this contact after they die. The question on this aspect in the interview is different from the question in questionnaire. The question in the interview is an open one while the question in the questionnaire is a closed one and the given answers are very limited. It is as same as the result when people talk about ancestors, only a few people associated descendants with the sacred world. Most people talk about it in this world.

3.4 Small Summary

To summarize the people's beliefs in the relationship between the living and the dead from the view of those whose self given identities are religious: (1) The dead relatives are still living somewhere because their souls are there. (2) It is a reality if the dead relatives appear in front of people. It can only occur when the heart of the living people is there. (3) The ancestors are immortals like God. God is regarded as a charismatic supernatural being but ancestors are not given the nature of God. This does not certainly mean that ancestors lost their supernatural characteristics from the view of some Chinese people. (4) The descendants the same as their parents are created by God. Both parents and children are independent individuals. Their relationship is relatively mutually independent.

The relationship between the living and the dead from the view of those whose self given identities are not religious: (5) The dead relatives are finished with their life and have left this world forever. It is just like everyone will die and vanish from the society in the end. (6) The dead people will never exist in reality after death. They can only remain in people's memories. They may appear in one's mind, for example in dreams, but it is a fantasy. (7) The ancestors or God have no power over humans because ancestors died and God never existed in the world. The so called power comes from what the ancestors did when they were alive not from what the ancestors do after they die. (8) The descendants are the next generation of the humans. The relationship between generations is complex. People have different views about the meaning of their younger generation growing. In general there are two types. One is the relationship of a chain, meaning the older generation has permanent connection with the younger even if they die. The other is the relationship of a relay, meaning everyone walks through one section of the whole human's history.

4. Interaction with Strangers

The questions about interaction with strangers in the interview are: "Being a stranger in a place which you do not know, how do you usually associate with others at the beginning?" "To see a stranger in a place which you are familiar, how do you usually associate with him or her at the beginning?" These two questions are compatible with the questions in the questionnaire. The only difference is that the questions in the questionnaire are situational. The strangers are mainly referred to colleagues in working place and students in a university. The questions in the interview do not have that limitation. The strangers might be anyone whom you do not know. The changes of the situations are being a stranger in a strange place (a new company or a new city, and so on) and seeing a stranger in a familiar place (a new neighbour or a new colleague).

4.1 Being a Stranger in a Strange Place

The interview results about how people usually associate with others in terms of being a stranger in a strange place show that most people would like to get close to others initiatively. They usually take the first step. The ways they get close to others are simply to go to others directly, or to get close to others step by step. The people whom they like to get close to are those who are friendly, open minded, and interesting. It depends on both their personal taste and the behaviour of the opposite side. The reason they get close to others is to fulfill the needs in themselves. This result was reported in chapter three as an example of the argument that questionnaire and interview cannot be replaced one another. Some people prefer to wait passively for others to come to them. The reasons for doing it this way are that they feel a little shy if they talk to others first, or they think that it is more polite to wait for others to talk to them first. Things will be much easier for them if others talk to them first. Some people said that it depends. They want to distinguish between different groups and different individuals. In a working place, colleagues have work contact; In a club, members have the same hobby; In a cafeteria, things will be complicated. It means that it is easier for colleagues in the same company or members in a same club to contact each other and it is more difficult for the customers in a cafeteria to contact each other. For the individuals, they like to get close to those who are friendly, helpful, and amiable. Few people said that they would like keep distance from others. It shows no difference from the results from the questionnaire (See Table 36).

To compare the answers of the four groups, the people who are in the two religious groups take more initiative than the people who in the two non religious groups. The people who are in the two German groups take more initiative than the people who are in the two Chinese groups. Though many people said that they would get close to others when being a stranger, some of them seem more open, some of them seem relatively cautious (See Example 31-36).

Table 36: Being a Stranger How Associate with Others

	German Religious	German non Religious	Chinese Religious	Chinese non Religious	Total
Get Close Initiatively	3	3	4	1	11
Wait Others Passively	3	1	0	3	7
Depends on Cases	2	5	4	3	14

Example 31: This is an example of those who like to get close to others directly in order to get help from others. "I would like to communicate with others to get help from them. I remember the first day I came to Germany. That was the first time I came to a foreign country. According to my thinking, there must be someone who was waiting for me at the airport because I had sent fax to my professor and told him the arrival time. But I did not see anyone who came to me after I got off the plane. What bad luck, I thought. At this moment, the woman who sat next to me on the plane came to me. After she knew everything, she offered me a help initiatively. She helped me to change money and then drove me to my working place. Her help impressed me very deeply. From my own experience, I know that I need to contact people if I am a stranger and strangers need help."

"I found later that there are many differences between the Germans and the Chinese. People can take the bus without their tickets being checked. People can buy news paper by putting coins willingly. Why do the Germans have this consciousness? I asked. "Because they have religious beliefs" is what I found. I did not know much about religion in the past. Friends took me to a Chinese religious society. I think that it is a good group. From there I know that the religious believers believe that everything they do is to win the honour for God. I experienced it more and more."

Example 32: This is an example of those who like to get close to others when they go to a new place but step by step. "First I try to understand the structures of the people, their relationship. Then I try to adapt in the same way but do not change myself. I try to approach those whom I think are similar because I need to have a certain relationship with people. Then I see if it works well or not so well because I cannot do all at once. I must find out what are the rules of people in different groups to establish their network."

"I have been in China. I cannot speak Chinese. I found out that usually I could not communicate with people in the street, no way. But the situation is different in the university. Some of them, not all of them, can speak English. Even if they cannot, they sometimes pretended that they can. Even I speak English with them, sometimes I did not understand what they mean. I try to find out how they felt and what they meant. Actually, I did not have any ideas before. It is very interesting to find that the students in China are very much like the students in Germany. The differences between the young people and the old people in the same country are more than the differences between the students in China and the students in western countries. I believe that human beings have something in common: we need love, friendship all over the world."

Example 33: This is an example of those who prefer to wait for somebody to come to them because they feel a little shy if they talk to somebody first. "I am more passive than active when I go to a new place. I wait until someone talk to me. It is not often that I start talking to others. I am at the boarder. I am a little shy. My mind is open to them. I trust them. I am not negative. I do not think that they are not friendly. I think about them positively but I hesitate to be active."

Example 34: This is another example of those who prefer wait until somebody comes to them because they think that things will be easier in that way. "It is too complicated for me to contact others first if I am in a strange place. I am open. I am always glad if somebody comes to me and speaks to me first. That makes things much easier for me. I do not think that I am too shy. It depends very much on other people. (Ask: how do you make a judgement about others?) It is what I feel. It is hard to tell how you judge but how you feel. It is mixture, their speaking, their body language, their facial expression, their general appearance."

Example 35: This is an example of those who want to distinguish different groups when they go to a new place. "It depends on what people they belong to. If it is in a working place, we are colleagues. It is easy and quick for me to get close to them because of our working relationship. If it is in others places, people who have common hobbies, have common topics, for example, sports or music, they are also easy to associate. It is not only that you need to talk to them and also that they need to talk to you. As to other people, it needs a period of time and a process of knowing each other, from the beginning of first meeting to the later interaction."

Example 36: This is an example of those who want to distinguish different individuals when they go to a new place. "Some people make good impression on you, you like to get close to them. Some people make bad impression on you, you think that you had better keep distance to them. You can make a judgement from simple aspects. (Ask: what are the simple aspects?) It is hard to say. It depends on his attitude to you. It is not a hundred per cent correct but about right."

"If somebody is very nice and warm, you would like get close to her; If somebody is impolite and cold, you will keep distance to her. My first household, only one year older than me, helped me a lot. She asked me initiatively if I need help. We are still good friends now. Of course, sometimes you should be careful. If a stranger comes to me and talk, I would ask, what is behind? (Ask: how do you make a judgement?) It is hard to say. It depends on my life experience. Most people here are good people. I would be very happy generally if somebody helps me initiatively."

4.2 Seeing a Stranger in a Familiar Place

The investigation results about how people usually associate with others if they see strangers in a familiar place show that most people would like to get close to the strangers because they want to know them and offer them help. They want to get necessary information from the strangers by getting to know them. They like to help the strangers because they themselves had the experience of being a stranger. Some of them prefer waiting for the strangers to ask them something first because they do not know what the strangers need and they themselves have no need to know the strangers. It is interesting to see that somebody said that it is much easier for them to talk to a stranger in a familiar place than to talk to a stranger in a strange place. It is also interesting to see that somebody said that they take the initiative to get close to strangers when they are in a strange place while they need not to take that initiative when they are in a familiar place. Some people said: it depends. They want to see if others really have needs and what are the needs. If others need a help, they will help them. If they have no need, why do something extra? On the other hand, they want to see what impression they make on them and how much sympathy they feel and how much they are interested in them. It also depends on their personal experience, positive or negative. Few people said that they would like to keep distance from others or to avoid other's company. It shows no difference from the results of the questionnaire (See Table 37).

Table 37: Seeing a Stranger How Associate with Him

	German Religious	German non Religious	Chinese Religious	Chinese non Religious	Total
Get Close Initiatively	7	5	5	4	21
Wait Others Passively	0	2	2	2	6
Depends on Cases	1	2	1	1	5

To compare the answers of the four groups, most people would like to get close to the strangers in the place which they are familiar. There are not many differences in behaviour but the motives behind the behaviour are different. When explaining it from the view of religion, as one of the interviewees said, to get close to the strangers and help them is to win the honour for God. When explaining it from the need of people, to get close to the strangers and help them is to meet the needs of the strangers and to fulfil the curiosities of the people. When explaining it from the view of custom, to get close to the strangers and help them is a polite way of being a host to a guest (See example 37-40).

Example 37: This is an example of those who would like to get close to the strangers because they know that strangers may need their help. "I try to get to know him. I start talking to him. I would ask: Where are you from? What are you doing here? I can imagine that he must be not easy. I would say to him:

Come to me if you need help. I also introduce myself to him. It is a normal way for a host to a guest. Strangers need some necessary information, for example, where is the bank, shop, post. If he is my new colleague, he must want to know the facilities in the laboratory, the reference in the library."

Example 38: This is an example of those who think that it is easier to talk to a stranger in a familiar place than talk to a stranger in a new place. "That will be easier for me, for example, at work. I try to be friendly to my new colleague. If someone in the street asks me the way, I tell him and help him. I try to be more open. I would say to myself: if I go to a new place, I would be a little bit but not too shy. If I am in that situation, I hope people come to me and help me. So I try that way."

Example 39: This is an example of those who prefer waiting for the strangers asking them something first because they do not know what they need, perhaps they do not need anything at all. "It is interested for me to see what they want. Maybe he or she needs help but I am very careful because I do not want to approach this person if the person does not want to. Maybe other people already helped this person. I do not want to do too much. So I am careful to find out what he or she wants."

Example 40: This is an example of those who think that they have no need to get close to the strangers definitely in a place which they are familiar. "It is completely different in the situation of a familiar place from in the situation of a strange place. Once in your own context, maybe it is not so necessary to get close to those people. I just say: Hello. As the time pass by, I will know them naturally. I may meet a lot of strangers in different places, I need not to come to them one by one."

4.3 Small Summary

To summarized the interaction with strangers: (1) Most people would like to get close to others when being a stranger in a stranger place though some of them take more initiative and some of them are relatively passive. The reason that they get close to others is to win the honour for God and to fulfil their needs, the needs of working, the needs of living, or psychological needs. (2) Most people would like to get close to strangers when seeing a stranger in a familiar place. Again, some of them take more initiative and some of them are relatively passive. Some people who take initiative when being strangers seem relatively passive when seeing a stranger. Some people who are relatively passive when being a stranger become initiative when seeing a stranger. The changes along with the changes of the situation may explain why those people take initiative sometimes and are passive some other times. The individuals' needs and their personal characters might be the influential factors. (3) If the above active communication or interaction among the strangers is regarded as positive, it can be attributed to wining the honour for God from the view of religion, it can be attributed to fulfilling the needs of people from the realistic attitude, it can be attributed to interaction orientation from the view of psychology and sociology. The word "need" were used more often than the others by the interviewees.

4.4 Special Topic: Love at First Sight

To investigate the interaction between strangers, two additional questions were raised: "If a man and woman fall in love at first sight or divorce after living together for many years, how do you explain it?" "Two persons like old friends at the first meeting or know each other for a long time but fight often, how do you explain it?" To compare these two questions with the similar questions in the questionnaire, some contents are added in the interview. Each of the two questions contains the meaning of falling in love and being friends but also contains the meaning of divorce and fight (not to associate well). The purpose of the questions is to ask people the views on how people love each other and how they maintain the relationship.

The interview results about the first question show that some people believe that falling in love at first sight is because of fate. The concept of fate from their view is the relation between cause and effect. It means that nothing can happen without a cause. In Buddhism it is called Karma. What one did in the previous life decides his fate in the future life. In Chinese the substitute word is called Yuanfen. It means good luck by which people are brought together. Some people believe in Yuanfen but cannot explain clearly what it is. They said: if two persons meet and are congenial, it means that two have Yuanfen. If two persons meet but are not congenial, it means that they do not have Yuanfen. The three terms fate, Karma and Yuanfen are not completely the same. Fate stresses destiny. Karma stresses cause and effect. Yuanfen stresses luck. But people use them interchangeably. Most people think that falling in love at first sight is because of other reasons. It might be attraction, good looking, wit saying, which make people be interested in each other. It might be emotion, the right time, the right place, which arouses in men and women an enthusiasm. It also might be congruence, meaning the one whom they imagined in their mind appears in front of them. Some people think that falling in love at first sight is because of both fate and other reasons. If one can meet this person rather than that person, it is because of fate. If one loves this person after they meet, it is because of other reasons. Some people gave some comments about the statement: It is possible to fall in love at first sight but this love is only on the surface. It seems that the two attract each other but in fact they are incompatible. It is hard to say that if it is a love everlasting and unchanging or if it is a flash in the pan. Feeling is built up by the interaction between the two persons.

As to the divorce, some people believe that it is also because of fate just the same as falling in love at first sight. People who have this belief normally do not say exactly what cause precedes the effect but they believe that it must result from something in the past, or they believe that people themselves cannot decide how their relationship develops, something just happens in a way that cannot be resisted then Yuanfen is finished. Most people think that there are many factors leading to divorce. The foundation of marriage is not solid, somebody selected a wrong partner at the beginning, for example, a flash marriage without enough understanding, high expectation before the marriage then much disappointment. Something changed after the marriage among the two persons, for example, changes of feelings (be tired of each other), changes of life (work change, child birth). Neglect to cultivate the relationship after marriage (busy with each own affairs). A third person pushes into a queue out of turn. Some people think that it is because of both fate and other factors. They said that they believe in fate and at the same time they gave other explanations as well. Some people gave some comments about the statement again: Falling in love at first sight is different category from divorce. Falling in love at first sight may or may not be a beginning of an intimate relationship. Divorce is the end of an intimate relationship (See Example 41-46).

Example 41: This is an example of those who believe that falling in love at first sight or divorce after living together for many years because of fate. "It is possible that a man and a woman fall in love at first sight. We have a law of Karma. It means everything has a cause. Everything that we do or everything that happens to us is the cause of our action which we acted in the previous life or this life. With all the people we meet, there is a reason. (Ask, what are the reasons for us to meet today?) For us, I do not know. It is possible that we meet also in another life by the law of Karma. The case that a man and a woman divorced after living together for many years is different. The teaching of Karma can explain everything possibly. My parents divorced. I think probably the relationship between my mother and my father is also by Karma. They can get through the life for a certain period of time but for their own development, they need different people to relate to. They have to stop their relationship. They could not really control the development themselves any longer."

Example 42: This is another example of those who believe that falling in love at first sight or divorce after living together for many years because of fate. "Fall in love at first sight? It is possible. Is it reliable? It needs to be tested. It is a kind of Yuanfen. (Ask: what is Yuanfen?) Yuanfen is a process from cause to effect. Yuan is cause. Yuanfen is good luck by which people are brought together, it is effect. Nowadays, people use these terms carelessly. Yuan and Yuanfen are lumped together. Divorce has also its reasons. In this case, Yuan is the time of the sustention of a relationship between a man and a woman. It is like a time of keeping quality of food. When it exceeds the time limit, the Yuanfen is over. Why is there a time limit? It is because of a combination of all kinds factors. Once the combination is destroyed, things will change, from one effect to another, that is divorce."

Example 43: This is an example of those who think that falling in love at first sight or divorce after living together for many years is because of other factors. "It is possible. I read a very interesting article in a magazine. It is said that a man and a woman may fall in love at first sight. There must be a media between the two people, for example, when something around them is moving. There was a woman who did an interview, like you are doing now. She interviewed a man on a bridge. When the bridge is shaking or rocking, the two people's hearts started moving. As to divorce, it is very complicated. If the two people divorced after living together for several years, then it must be one or two lost his or her beliefs in the relationship. It is not just the loss of love but the confidence in love is missing. That is something you can deal with in your mind in your heart. One or two of them do not work with it anymore, then separate."

Example 44: This is another example of those who think that falling in love at first sight or divorce after living together for many years because of other factors. "It is possible. It is because that someone has been brewing for a long time, then one day he has the opportunity. The lover in dreams appears before the eyes. It just meets his needs. So the relationship may develop very fast. Divorce, it is because the feelings have broken up. Perhaps they are not compatible originally. They get married before the relationship is mature. They did not realize the existence of the risk until the day the potential problem intensified. Feeling is something relative rather than absolute. If feeling has its life, it needs to be looked after. Otherwise, it may die."

Example 45: This is another example of those who think that falling in love at first sight or divorce after living together for many years because of other factors. "It is an interesting question. It is possible to fall in love at first sight. If you pay attention to, you may see many examples of those people who just look at each other for a while without talking who can get ideas about like or dislike the opposite side. It might be the way a person smiles, a gesture a person makes, or even the smell a person "sends out". In fact, you cannot smell anything, it is a feeling, a feeling of confidence and comfortable. Divorce? Yes, it may happen in every relationship. It seems wonderful at the beginning but in fact you found a wrong person originally. People have different experience may have different values, different habits. They may develop in different direction."

Example 46: This is an example of those who believe that falling in love at first sight or divorce after living together for many years because of both fate and other reasons. "It is a good question. I gave the answer that I need to see the special case. I think that it is because of both fate and attraction. It just depends. It is because of fate if there was an encounter in the past life. Karma is the expression in eastern philosophy. Fate is the expression in western philosophy. In German "Schicksal", refers to the law of cause and effect. I believe in reincarnation but not in the same way of living, maybe in another way. This is my Karma. It is possible to fall in love at first sight. For example, you and I met in an earlier life, not our persons but our mind or our soul. If fall in love because of fate, then divorce also because of fate. Of course, there are other reasons which may result in love and divorce. Feeling, feeling is a changeable factor, for example."

The interview results about the second question show that some people believe that two persons feel like old friends at first meeting because of fate. They believe that there is nothing in the world which is accidental. To look back the life in the past, it must have a deep background. Perhaps it is not the first meeting of the two persons. They met already previously. He or she comes today with his or her incarnation. Most people think that they feel like old friends at the first meeting because of other reasons, in general, the similarities between each other. They may have similar interests, they can share their interests. They may have similar thoughts, similar view of life, similar values. They may have similar feelings, one loves what the other loves, one hates what the other hates. They may have similar backgrounds, similar families, similar educations. They may have similar dispositions. Some people think that they feel like old friends at first meet because of both fate and other reasons. These two persons not others meet because of fate. What they did in the past life decides their meeting in this life. Two persons find each other congenial because of similar tastes and interests. Some people think that it is impossible to feel that a stranger is like an old friend at first meeting because all of those who became friends experienced a period of time, many times of meeting, many times contact. How can people be friends without understanding?

As to conflict, some people believe that it is also because of fate. The two persons may fight for many lives. They meet again and again. One may come to this world in order to get something back from the other or to requite ingratitude from the other. Most people think that two persons who have known each other for a long time but fight each other often is because of other reasons, in general, the differences between each other. They have different thinking, different beliefs which is difficult for them to have common sense. They have different understanding about each other which make them feel difficult or impossible to interact. They have different dispositions which make them dislike or annoy one another. They may have had bad experiences which make them stereotype the other person is bad. They have different benefit which results in fight. Some people think both fate and other reasons. For example, both people are aggressive and different, they are just arranged by fate to meet each other (See Example 47-52).

Example 47: This is an example of those who believe that to feel like old friends at first meeting or know each other for many years but fight often is because of fate. "This happens to me. I am sure that it is due to the Karma of us. I believe that we probably met in the past life, now we meet again. This is why we are so close to each other. I have no explanations but this. I can tell you a nice example. One of my friends, a monk, he met with another monk in the street, a stranger. They had different robes, my friend had orange robe, the other had brown robe. They noticed each other about 100 meter, they ran to each other and embraced each other. It is clear to them that they had met each other before and now they met again. Conflict, it is possible. It is because they are enemies for many lives. They meet again and again. It is also by the arrangement of Karma. It is not good to fight but things turned out just the opposite."

Example 48: This is another example of those who believe that to feel like old friends at first meeting is because of fate. "Nothing in the world is accidental. Cause and effect circulate in the three lives, previous life, present life, and future life. You may not see the reasons around you but you will find it if you see your previous life. I have a good friend here whom I knew in a class. We just had a class together in one semester, we became good friends. There are many classmates whom I have known for two or three years but I even do not want to say hello to them."

"Good encounter must have reasons. The sunshine, water, soil, all of these conditions become mature, it means that the reasons become enough, the fruit will grow or the chance will come. Otherwise, the good encounter may not happen between these two persons. If they do not have a good relationship, they fight each other often, it must have reasons as well. One must have one or a few of the four relationships with others: to get something back from others, to pay his debt to others, to pay a debt of gratitude, or to requite ingratitude. Once one finishes doing what he needs to do, he finishes his relationship."

Example 49: This is an example of those who think that to feel like old friends at first meeting or know each other for many years but fight often because of other reasons. "I think that they feel like old friends at first meeting, they must find a common topic, they must have the similar experiences, they like the same things and hate the same. They understand each other. If they know each other for many years but fight often, they must have different experience, they cannot understand each other well, like a square peg in a round hole."

Example 50: This is another example of those who think that to feel like old friends at first meeting or know each other for many years but fight often because of other reasons. "It comes from the same feeling, the same sympathy. Feeling is something, when I make a joke, you know, you laugh. I know you from your laugh that you and I have the same humour. So I like you. As to the conflict, some people are more "struggle" while some people are more peaceful. The struggle man likes fighting while the peaceful man always tries to avoid it."

Example 51: This is an example of those who think that to feel like old friends at first meeting or know each other for many years but fight often because of both fate and other reasons. "Some people told me the one you feel like old friend at first meeting is an incarnation. You might meet him in another life in the past. Another explanation is that you and that person have similar thinking. It happens again and again. Usually I can trust my feelings. It gives me courage. If you do not know somebody, you may feel dangerous to open yourself up too much. If two persons know each other for many years but "fight" often, it might be that they are together on the wrong basis. They do not really understand each other. Maybe they are together for material, for property purposes, they have conflict, it is normal."

Example 52: This is an example of those who think that it is impossible to feel that a stranger is like an old friend at first meeting because all of those who became friends experienced a period of time to get to know one another. How can people be friends without understanding? "No, I think that it is impossible. All good friends of mine are those whom I met many times. Maybe some people explain it from the view of religion, that they have been friends in their former life, but I do not believe it. It never happened to me. I always need time to know a person and to make friends with him or her. If two persons know each other for many years but fight often, it is possible. They are different type of human beings. They cannot go together. They have something which makes the other annoy, angry. If you meet with that kind of people, you just let them do."

5. Interaction with Intimates

The questions about interaction with intimates in the interview are: "To contact with your partner or the intimates, do you often tell him or her about your private thoughts? Do you often express your feelings to him or her?" "To contact with your partner or the intimates, can you share interests with him or her? Can you understand him or her as much as you can?" To compare the questions about the interaction with strangers, these questions are more specific. These questions include different components of intimacy. The questions about the interaction with strangers are completely open. People can answer them from any angle. The first two questions about interaction with intimates are about sharing behaviour. The next two questions about interaction with the intimates are about sharing experience. All the answers for these four questions can be categorized into two kinds: One is "Yes, I do"; The other is "It depends". The above table shows that the answers "Yes, I do" on each of the four questions (See Table 38).

Table 38: Share with the Intimates

	German Religious	German non Religious	Chinese Religious	Chinese non Religious	Total
Disclose Thoughts	5	7	6	5	23
Express Feelings	3	7	6	2	18
Share Interests	6	7	5	5	23
Understand Others	7	7	7	5	26
Total Cases	8	9	8	8	32

5.1 Share Behaviour with Intimates

The interview results about self disclosure with intimates show that most people would like to lay bare their thoughts to their intimates, to tell their intimates what they think and what is going on, because they want to exchange ideas with them and to get advice from them. They think that people should trust each other among the intimates. The intimates might be their partner, their parents, their siblings, or their friends. Whom they talk to depends on the structure of their intimates' network, who is the closest one to him or her in the net who is the object to talk. Many people said that they usually talk more to their partners or friends than to their parents or siblings. Some people said that they do not tell everything to their intimates. It depends on the contents of their thoughts. There are some contents which they only talk to their partners or friends. There are some contents which they can talk to their parents or siblings. There are some contents on which they need to speak out because they need to communicate with intimates. There are some contents on which they had better hold back because telling them to the intimates may result in bad consequences. It does not mean that they are not honest (See Example 53-56).

Example 53: This is an example of those who like to tell their intimates what they think and what is going on. "I live together with my parents. I often tell them what is going on. I trust them. I would not tell them everything but the main things because I want to communicate with them. If I could not solve some problems myself, I would ask them, their opinions. I like to discuss with those who are familiar to me. It is helpful for me and it is also good for them to know."

Example 54: This is another example of those who like to exchange ideas with their intimates. "I talk with my husband often. It is interesting that I talk about my affairs and he talks about his. He is a business man and I am a teacher. In fact, I am not very interested in the business affaires but I still try to listen to. I make some suggestions to him sometimes, hit the mark by a fluke, it works. He is not familiar with my field but he also gives me some advice. The environment in my working place is depressed. There are many words which I cannot say there. To talk about it after work at home, I feel comfortable."

Example 55: This is an example of those who do not tell everything to their intimates, it just depends. "I can tell my best friends about my own thinking when I get good feelings. Sometimes, even to my best friends, I do not tell at all. I am not a open book which others can read from page to page, they can read a little bit, that is all (hey, hey, smile). This is good, I think. If you have a friend over five or ten years, you need not talk much. He knows what you mean by checking your face."

Example 56: This is another example of those who do not tell everything to their intimates, it would be better not to say. "I need to think about it. I talked everything in the past. Now I grow up, become mature, I do not say everything casually. To say those which I should say. (Ask: why did you have this change?) I think more and become more complicated. Sometimes I do not want to say because I cannot explain it clearly, the more I explained, the more it is confused. Let it pass. Everybody has everybody's internal world, different experience, different thinking. It is not necessary to express all of my world to others."

The interview results about emotional expression with intimates show that some people would like to express their feelings anyway because they need to express it and their intimates want to know it as well. It is a behaviour which people need not to think about much, but to give vent to their angry, to share the joy of their goodness. They think that people need not control much among the intimates. Of course, there are many kinds of feelings. Some feelings are easier to express, some feelings are more difficult to express. For example, it is easier to express "positive" feelings, such as happiness and love. It is more difficult to express "negative" feelings, such as anxiety and angry. As to sadness, different people have different opinions. Some people said that they do not want to express their feelings much. To control themselves as much as they can, if it is not able to bear, then let it off (See Example 57-59).

Example 57: This is an example of those who would like to express their feelings anyway. "Everybody knows that I am in good spirits or not. I think that feeling is part of the human beings. I want to have it and let people see that I have it. I do not want to terrorize others with anger, or something. But once you have this feeling, you need not have it in mind. I do want people to feel my feelings. I am a human being. I have right to express it. If I have not feelings, I have no way to interact you."

Example 58: This is another example of those who would like to express their feelings anyway. "I express my feelings, every kind of feeling, to my husband often. We both do. I hope so. We had some hard time because of job problem, change places, and so on. We talked about it even it was a little bit hard. It was very important that we talk about our feelings in that situation. Afterwards, when everything was OK, we were happy, we talked about being happy. Every time, when there is a change in the surrounding, concerning the job, whatever, we talk about. It is helpful for us to make a decision."

Example 59: This is an example of those who do not want to express their feelings much. To control, if it is not able to bear, then let it off. "I do not express my feelings often. I like to express my opinions. To be more objective is more important for me. I do not think that I can express my feelings well. I am normally very calm. If someone makes me angry, for example, I am too angry to control, I will let it off."

5.2 Share Experience with Intimates

The interview results about sharing interests with the intimates show that most people can share interests with their intimates. They either have the same interests with their intimates because the same interests brought them together, or they are interested in each other interests because they are curious about them and by enjoy others' interests they can increase others' enjoyment. Some people said that they can only share some of the interests with their intimates, for example, one person is a sociologist, one person is a business man, they cannot share each others subjects (See Example 60-62).

Example 60: This is an example of those who like to share the interests with their intimates because it is interesting. "I like very much to share interests with others because I am a person who is interested in everything. I have a friend, about his hobby, his work, I do not know at all, but I like to discuss with him, for example, what he reads and what he does. His interests are not mine but talking with him itself is interesting. I would like to try what he likes sometimes."

Example 61: This is another example of those who enjoy others' interests because it can increase others' enjoyment. "I enjoy others' interests. Others will be happy of being enjoyed. Sometimes, even if I am not interested in their interests, I still pretended to be interested in them, to say something, to help them thinking. If somebody shows you a "masterpiece" which he made, you do not even have a look. How does he feel? If somebody invites you to eat in a special restaurant, you do not enjoy. How does he feel?"

Example 62: This is an example of those who can only share some of the interests with their intimates or have difficulty to share with them. "My closest person is my husband. But his interests are completely different form mine. I do not force him to have the same interests as mine. He has his own freedom. He can do what he likes. I have my own things to do. I do not want others to interfere me. Sometimes I may listen to his opinions. I also tell him mine no matter he accepts it or not."

The interview results about understanding between the intimates show that most people try to understand their intimates because they think that they cannot interact with each other without understanding. This is also the most identical point from the results of the questionnaire. Of course, misunderstanding may happen sometimes or often. Sometimes one person tries to understand another but he or she is not sure if his or her understanding is right. So they need more communication. Some people think that it is ok if they can understand each other; it is also good if they cannot. Some people said that they sometimes have different opinions from others and they think that their opinion is more reasonable. So they need to talk to others and hope that others can understand them (See example 63-66).

Example 63: This is an example of those who try to understand their intimates as much as they can but in fact, just to a certain degree. "I try to understand them as much as I can. But the result is that I can only understand them in a certain degree. If the two persons are too different, I doubt that they can understand each other. If the two persons have common characters, it is possible. It is a challenge. There are some limitations to understand them. But I always try to put myself into the mind of others to think about them. One of my favourite job is to be an actor. Being an actor, you need to understand what you are acting. So to try to understand others is important."

Example 64: This is another example of those who try to understand their intimates as much as they can but it seems difficult. "I want to understand the opposite side but it seems difficult. Misunderstanding happens often. We do not have bad intention to hurt each other but the result is that one is hurt. In this situation, I would try to explain: I did not mean that. But I found that some people do not want to discuss at all and say: let it pass. I have no opportunity to make a dialogue. I want to argue that both of us did not have bad intention. Of course, there are some bad persons do something bad on purpose. I want to test it. I like to seek for harmony."

Example 65: This is an example of those who sometimes have different opinions from others and they think that their opinion is more reasonable. So they need to talk to others and hope that others can understand them. "Sometimes I have different opinions from others. I have my own way of thinking. It is not that I do not understand them but they do not understand me. Then I need to explain. I must explain it, otherwise I feel uncomfortable. So we say that we try to understand each other, we do not say that we only try to understand others. Others should also understand me. "

Example 66: This is an example of those who think that it is ok if they can understand each other; it is also good if they cannot. "If a person is different from me, I find even more interesting. If a person is similar to me, I know it too much. Then I may feel dull. I am interested in people who are different because it is fascinating in different thinking. (Ask: are there some misunderstandings happen?) Yes, all the time. You said something just like you usually say, the other person may understand you completely differently. Even your close friends, you need to understand him or her from time to time. Then you always have a new or fresh experience."

5.3 Small Summary

To summarize the interaction with the intimates: (1) Most people would like to share behaviour with their intimates, to present their thoughts to the intimates and to express their feelings to the intimates. To present their thoughts to the intimates or to express their feelings, they can get feedback from the opposite side. This feedback can be an advice or a suggestion or just a listening. However, some people think that to present their thoughts does not mean that they do not hold back at all. To express feelings does not mean that they do not control. To hold back those thoughts which may result in trouble and to control those feeling which may have negative effects is necessary in the interaction with the intimates. (2) Most people would like to share experience with their intimates, to share interests with their intimates and to understand their intimates. Sharing interests can be in the form of doing something together or in the form of talking about interests to each other. Understanding between the intimates is the most identical point in the investigation. The precise expression of understanding between the intimates from the interview is to try to understand others instead of to be able to understand others because the uncertainty or misunderstanding may happen sometimes or often. It makes the interaction between the intimates mysterious and complicated. It is not only the identical point from the view of the interviewees but also the key point of interaction from the view of sociology. (3) To compare the answers of the four groups, there are not many differences. To compare the answers of these questions with the answers of other questions, the answers of these questions by people are brief and short.

5.4 Special Topic: Parents Bring up Children

To investigate the interaction between the intimates, two additional questions were raised: "For what purposes do parents bring up children? Is it important for one to have children?" "Why do parents expect children to become useful persons? Is it meaningful for the parents themselves?" These two questions are also as same as the questions in the questionnaire. As it mentioned in the preceding chapter, the given answers in the questionnaire are not sufficient. The given answers are just some examples "to cast a brick to attract jade". It means to offer a few answers by way of introduction so that people may come up with their own opinions. But the same questions in the interview are completely open.

The interview results about the first question why parents bring up children show that people have different opinions. They each air their own views. To categorize those opinions into: for self, for society, and the nature of the humans. Those who think that bringing up children is for oneself said: To see children growing up is joys of life. To have children is to seek for love relationship. To have my livelihood assured when I am old. To leave something belonged to me in the world after I die. To have children itself is a kind of honour. Those who think to bring up children are for society said: to bring up children is a responsibility of parents. Those who think to bring up children is in the nature of humans said: It is a natural process of the human beings. Only to have children is the complete life of the humans. A baby is nothing but out of love. Just to have children without thinking or consideration.

Is it important for one to have children? Somebody said yes, somebody said no. Those who think that it is important for one to have children stated again the above reasons. All of them are out of the needs of themselves. Those who think that it is not important for one to have children gave their own reasons: I will loose my own freedom if I have children. Instead of taking care of one or two of my own children, I can educate a lot of other children. Woman had no choice in the past about their life but now I have right to choose to have or not to have children. It is difficult for me to listen to children crying around me. I need not to have children of my own because I have a lot of nephews and nieces. The society is over populated so I need not to add some additional. I have many friends with whom I have intimate relationship in stead of with my children. I want to development love relationship with God. I believe in reincarnation so my life will continue my self without children (See Example 67-71).

Example 67: This is an example of those who think that to bring up children is a responsibility of parents and the children can conversely take care of them when they become old. "To bring up children is our responsibility. You bring them up gradually, when they grow up, we are old, then the children can conversely take care of us. It is important to have children. It will be very lonely if one has not children. Children can take care of me if I am ill. Then you will be happy. For example, my sisters and I would go to see our parents every week. My parents would cook a lot of delicious food. We eat together. My father cooked very energetically. My mother said that it is worth spending money on it. She is very proud to say: You see, how my children show filial obedience. Neighbours admire us. We are happy."

Example 68: This is an example of those who think that a normal life of human beings should be in a way of bringing up children. "It is important. In our society, a normal life is to have a partner, then have a family, then bring up children. For women, to have children can make women feel that they are whole women because women have this ability. For man, the society expects them to have responsibility to the family, to work to make money for the family. It is very important for individuals to have children. Children are not something which you can buy. They are the humans whom you can have relationship with. I do not know if it is important for all people but it is also important for me because I am a woman. I want to feel that I am capable to have a baby. It makes me more complete. (Ask: why some people do not want to have children?) It is the problem now that some women think that it is more important for them to have a job. Many women study as well. They are quiet old when they start to work and they want to keep on working to keep on their career. For me, I think that it is more important to have a relationship with another human being than to have money in my bank account."

Example 69: This is an example of those who think that to bring up children is a biological matter and also can be a rational choice. "It is not that important. First of all, biological knowledge tells people to bring up children. Second, sometimes people want to leave something in the world after they die because they do not want to die. They do not do for the sake of children but for themselves. I have different opinions. It is ideal if you get married, then get pregnant, then you bring up children. But then, you are very stumpy. You cannot do your work well. You cannot go to other countries. (Ask: are you going to have a child?) No. I have a lot of nephews and nieces. I love them. That is really good. I love children. I thought about it and everyone should think about it. By the way, I just saw a study in Germany, 31% of academic women in Germany do not have children. (Ask: do you think that they are not willing to have or they are too busy to have?) It is not because that they are too busy to have. They can do both but they just have other interests."

Example 70: This is an example of those who believe that he can develop love relationship with friends and God instead of Children. "Everybody has a basic need of oneself. This need is the longing of love to other people. The longing for love relationship is there, whatever you live on it or not. This is the reason that people want to have children because they know that with a child they can have very intimate relationship. (Ask: do you want to have a child?) (Laugh......) Maybe not. It is possible that I stay myself in my life because I have somehow the feeling that I am not meant to marry this life. I do not feel the urge to have a partnership. Instead to have intimate relationship with a partner then with a child, I may have intimate relationship with God. For many people, it is important to have children. Right now, it is not so important for me. I am happy with my life. I have many friends who are religious. We try to develop personal relationship with God. Maybe I will have a child in the future but not now. (Ask: why is it important to have children for others?) Because they do not looking for a relationship with God. I think that the relationship with God can fulfil my desires. If you do not fulfil your desires by building a relationship with God, you build a relationship with other human beings."

Example 71: This is an example of those who believe that there will be a reincarnation after death. "Everybody has everybody's life. I think that to bring up children is not for material reasons in my case. It is enjoyable for being around by little kids. But I do not think that I will have children. It is not important for me. My life might be changed too much if I have children because I would have new responsibility. The little kid crying may change one's whole life. It is not desirable. Another reason that I do not want to have children is that there are over population in the world, too many people to give birth, even in Munich. I do not want to increase it anymore. (Ask: the population is not over surplus in Germany, especially children, isn't it?) Ya, but for me, is too much already. I do not like it. I see people rushing up to me in the downtown, it is very crowded in the subway. I feel very uncomfortable. The life would be more pleasant if there are fewer people. I believe in reincarnation. I do not need my children to extend my existence because my mind will be reincarnated. I do not want to have trouble raising children cost my energy, time for many years."

The interview results about the second question why parents place expectations on their children shows that they each have their own views. Those opinions can be categorized into: for oneself, for the children, and for society. Those who think that the purpose of placing expectations on children is for themselves said: Parents have high prestige if their children have money, have a good education. Parents will have a feeling of achievement if their children are very successful. Parents will feel comforted if their children are very independent. Parents will be fulfilled if their children make the parents' dreams come true. Parents' project of educating their children is tested by the success or failure of a child. Parents can rely on their children when they are old. Those who think that the purpose of placing expectations on children is for the children said: Parents have expectations of children because they hope their children have a happy life. Those who think that the purpose of placing expectations on children is for society said: Parents hope their children to be useful for society.

Is it meaningful for the parents themselves? Most people said yes, some people said no. Those who think that it is meaningful for the parents stated again the above reasons. It is a great comfort for the parents if the children are independent. Those who think that it is not meaningful for the parents gave their own reasons: What children will be is not determined by their parents but by themselves. Parents should not have any selfish ideas and personal considerations for their children. Children's lives are decided by their own fate which is not something that parents can do. To seek for God is the goal for every soul rather than what parents hope children to have (See Example 72-76).

Example 72: This is an example of those who think that parents have many expectations of their children because they hope their children can make the parents dreams come true. "Parents expect their children do something which the parents themselves could not do. They could not do that in their life so they want their children do that. My father always wants me to study. Maybe their generation had less opportunity to go to a university. But now many parents want their children have a nice life, be happy. They hope that their children have the job they want to have, get everything they want to get. My father is different from the younger fathers. Of course, it is meaningful for the parents themselves if their children are successful. They will be proud. But I do not think that it is good because it causes problems. Both the children and the parents will feel disappointed if the children did not do the way like the parents expected. I think that children should have their own life while parents can help them but not force them. Everybody is an independent individual."

Example 73: This is an example of those who think that parents have many expectations of their children because family taking care of family is still one form for the aged. "Once you have a grown up child and you get old, you can get help from your children if the social security system has not been so developed that everyone can benefit from it. Once the social economic situation develops, the social security system will develop as well. It is a difficult task. Family take care family is still one form for the aged to spend their old age. All the parents of the world are very proud when their children do the way the parents expected, the success."

Example 74: This is an example of those who think that parents can expect children to be useful persons but cannot force them. "I think that parents in Asia have too many expectations of their children. In Germany, parents are happy to see their children to be useful for the society but to be useful does not definitely mean outstanding. Of course, there are still some severe parents who force their children do this and that. In general, parents offer children opportunities, and tell children why they offer that, if the children do not like, they can do what they want. Parents hope children happy. For what purposes? For both the honour of themselves and for the society. Nobody hopes his children to be useless. If the children are useful, parents will also have a feeling of achievement. But it cannot attribute all to parents. It is children's achievement."

Example 75: This is an example of those who think that their own goal is completely different from their parents. "Maybe in most cases it is because of the parents' prestige. (Ask: what is high prestige in Germany?) People make a lot of money no matter what they do. People who are well-educated also have high prestige. This is what my father wants me to do. He hopes that I either earn a lot of money or become a doctor. If I am that person, he can tell others that my son is a doctor or a rich man. I do not want to say that it is bad but it is not a pure motive. (Ask: what do you want to be?) I do not have a desire to have a lot of money, to have a high position. (Ask: what is your goal in life?) It is a very intimate question. I try to seek my philosophy of religion. I follow the teachings of the holy description of it. The goal of life, according to the teachings, is to develop a personal relationship with God. If you strive for this goal, you do not care so much about wealth, position. Because as soon as you make some experience of this path, all those things they come to you. It is meaningful for the parents if their children are wealthy and famous. A father will be shamed if his son is a beggar. He will be proud if his son is a scholar or a rich man. It is natural to everyone. It is not useful for spiritual path, but it is a natural need of people."

Example 76: This is an example of those who believe that everybody, including one's children, their lives is decided by their own fate. "Parents hope their own children have a happy life. It is normal and natural. But what the result is good or bad is not determined by parents but by the children's own fate. I do not think that it is meaningful for parents if their children are good or bad. All those things I cannot discipline. All those things are decided by their own fate. If my child has a happy life and is very filial to me, that is my good luck. If my child is born for getting something from me, I have to pay. As parents, we should do something for children with heart and might no matter he or she wants to get something from me or pay something for me. This is our responsibility."

6. Dealing with Problems

The questions about dealing with problems in the interview are: "What do you usually do when you suffer setbacks?" "What do the obstacles result from in your life?" It aims to ask people problem solving strategies and attribution style and then proceed to see if there are some differences between the people who have religious beliefs and who have not religious beliefs.

6.1 Problem Solving

The interview results about dealing with problems can be categorized into four kinds. The first is to try to find ways to overcome the setbacks. People try to analyse the problems, to find some solutions. Some people would try to deal with it alone because they think that the setbacks result from themselves. They must overcome it by themselves. They think that the setbacks have nothing to do with others. Others are helpless. Some people would try to ask for help from others. They talk to others and hope to get ideas from others because they do not want to endure the sufferings alone and they need others' ideas as reference. The second is to try to adjust themselves psychologically. Some people try to calm down by staying alone, listening to music, reading books. Some people try to change attitude from negative thinking to positive thinking, from pessimistic to optimistic by thinking that bad fortune lurks within good and good fortune lurks within bad. Some people try to shift attention by going shopping, swimming or eating. The third is to pray God for help. They try to tell God the truth sincerely and hope to get help from God earnestly. There are a certain number of people who stepped into the door of a church or a temple because they need help from God. The fourth is to try to accept the setbacks and to forget about it when the setbacks seem not to be overcome. They said that the problems will be solved with the passage of time (See Example 77-80).

Example 77: This is an example of those who try to find ways to overcome the setbacks. "Try to overcome setbacks, on the one hand to overcome it psychologically, on the other hand to overcome it with your abilities. Sometimes you are lucky that you get help from others. It is normal to have setbacks. There is not a smooth way to achieve something which is true in life. Once you achieve it by making effort, you will feel it is valuable. (Ask: somebody may say: you pray then you will have good luck?) I will not do that. If somebody advises me to widen my field of vision, I will listen to it. If somebody advises me to pray for God, I will not listen to it. When you want to bring every positive factors into play to solve problems, someone says that you need not think that, everything is arranged by fate, that person is just like a demon, he advises you flinch, I hope that I will never meet that kind of person."

Example 78: This is an example of those who try to adjust themselves psychologically. "I prefer stay alone if I have setbacks, to close myself in the room listening to music or reading books. When I feel better after a period of time, I come out again. (Ask: does it mean that the problem is solved when you feel better?) No. Some problems cannot be solved at all, so you should not take a matter to heart. Sometimes you do something silly, you feel bad, you hide. Long time ago, when I was a little boy, I saw some people playing on the road side. I was very interested in it. I tried but I lost a lot. I felt that people surrounding me were looking at me. I could find no place to hide myself for shame. I went home without saying a word. My mother was shocked. She did not know what happened. I did not tell her anything, just wait the time passed slowly."

Example 79: This is an example of those who believe that God can help them. "I will try to find ways to solve problems. At the same time, I pray God. In my belief, there is a God who helps us and creates everything, who is supernatural. I would pray God, like a Christian believer, to help me when I have difficulties. (Ask: does it work?) Yes. God will help me because I believe it. That is my experience. A few years ago, I made a mistake through an oversight in my experiment. According to the theory, it must be failed. I wanted to do it again but there is no chemical reagent left. My boss was waiting for the result of the experiment. It was too urgent to wait the new chemical reagents come. What is to be done? I had no way but wait the result coming out with my heart in my mouth. I prayed. I said to God: please help if you really have supernatural power! It turned out that the experiment was successful. It means that God's power helped me, doesn't it?"

Example 80: This is an example of those who try to accept the setbacks and to forget about it when the setbacks seem not to be overcome. "Have setbacks? You understand me most. Laugh ...... The theoretical saying is to be calm, to look at bright side of things, never get into a dead end (to take unnecessary pains to study an insoluble problem). Everybody will have big problems, in marriage, family, children, work, and so on. Those problems are seemed not important for others but absolutely important for individuals. When I have setbacks, I would look for friends having a chat. I try not to think about it. I suffered a lot in the past. It was harmful for my health. Now I think that I was stupid at that time. Sometimes you suffer heavy losses, you should think: My bad luck! Forget it! Don't be angry, my health is important."

6.2 Attribution Style

The interview results about the question how to attribute obstacles can be categorized into four kinds. The first is to attribute to internal factors. The obstacles result from internal factors. Sometimes it is a problem that oneself did not expect, for example, to have not enough abilities, to be not very considerate, to do something wrong. Sometimes it is a problem which one asked for, for example, it may not be a problem if one did not want to do that, it may not be a problem when one did not think of that. The second is to attribute to external factors. Sometimes it is because other people do not cooperate, for example, in working relationships, in personal relationships. Sometimes it is because the environment is not advantage, for example, the disadvantages of economic situation, a natural disaster. Sometimes it is because some people play tricks, for example, to harm others in order to benefit oneself. The third is to attribute to fate or Karma. For example: It is what one should deserve. If all those which belong to one, one cannot avoid; If all those which do not belong to one, one cannot get. It relates to one's past behaviour. That is to say that anything good or bad results from internal factors. All are asked for by oneself. The fourth is to attribute to internal factors sometimes and external factors sometimes, for example, sometimes there are psychological problems, sometimes there are environmental problems. Or setbacks can be attribute to the combination of internal and external problems. External causes become operative through internal causes (See Example 81-84).

Example 81: This is an example of those who think that most obstacles result from internal factors. "Most troubles result from inside of people. Sometimes you want to do something but you failed because you did not fully prepare for it. Sometimes you did something but you did not succeed because you did not work hard enough. Sometimes you make effort but you also failed because your abilities are limited. Sometimes the situation outside is really bad but how do you react to it? Finally it depends on your own. If you want to be happy, you will be happy. If you often worry about, you will have problems."

Example 82: This is an example of those who think that all obstacles result from internal. "All kinds of suffering relate to our past behaviour. Everything that happens to us has a cause in our past life. For example, if I hurt somebody in the past, I will see soon that I receive reaction of that. This is a law of Karma. This is also said in the Bible, in all religious scripture. Whatever what happens to us, we should not be angry about it. We should tolerate because we are the cause of it. When we go to the toilet, we should not complain the smell because we ourselves made it."

Example 83: This is an example of those who attribute problems to external factors. "I do not think that I have psychological problems. As to the external, I think that there are some problems. Most of the problems can be solved by making effort. But some problems are seemed difficult. For example, in the working unit, someone always criticize others. It makes you feel uncomfortable. This uncomfortable obstacle is difficult to get rid of. I have no way but tolerate and keep avoiding. It is better to build a good relationship with colleagues. But working together with that kind of person, it is helplessness."

Example 84: This is an example of those who think that obstacles come from inside sometimes and sometimes outside. "I think that both aspects. Most obstacles result from inside. For example, some goals are too high to reach, if you want it, you ask for trouble for yourself. Some obstacles result from outside. For example, someone is not fair, someone stumble you secretly. All of those are possible. Most people are good. But there are some bad people anyway. Sometimes the internal and external factors affect us together. For example, I have a bad mood and others too, then a fight will be difficult to avoid."

7. Immortals and People

The questions about the immortals and the people in the interview are: "Sometimes when you do something, do you feel that your ancestors or god are watching you or do you feel that other people are watching you?" "Normally when you do something, do you pay more attention to others' evaluation or do you pay more attention to your own experience?" These two questions are exactly the same as the questions in the questionnaire. In the preceding chapter, two questions were raised after the analysis of the data: One is that what is the interaction between the immortals and the people if the immortals are regarded as the significant others? The other is what is the relationship among oneself, other people, the immortals, and the business?

7.1 Who is Watching You

The interview results about the question who is watching you when you do something can be categorized into four kinds. The first is that some people feel that people are watching them regardless if those people are really watching them or not. It is an intrapersonal communication: How do others think about me? How do others judge me? For example: wearing a bizarre dress may feel ill at ease, buying something without paying may feel upset, hurting somebody may feel guilty. It is because everybody lives in a society not in an island. Social values and norms have effects on individuals by the eyes of mass. The second is that some people feel that God is watching them. They feel that God sees everybody. The eyes of God have a binding force. It can make people give up selfish ideas and personal considerations. The eyes of God have also a gravitational force. It can make people follow the law of God. These two forces will function once the concept of God is internalised by people, it will make people examine their conscience. The third is that some people feel that both people and God are watching them. This feeling sometimes appears alternatively sometimes appears simultaneously. The fourth is that some people said that nobody is watching them. They just do what they need to do. They feel free and unrestrained. They do everything with conscience. To compare the answers of the four groups, only the people in the religious groups may notice the presence of God. But not all the people in the religious groups have this consciousness. The people in the non religious groups only realize the presence of man or only concentrate on the things what they do (See Table 39 and Example 85-88).

Table 39: Who is Watching You

	German Religious	German non Religious	Chinese Religious	Chinese non Religious	Total
People	3	4	1	3	11
God	1	0	3	0	4
Both	1	0	1	0	2
Nobody	3	5	3	4	15

Example 85: This is an example of those who feel that people are watching them. "I think that it might be people who are watching me. They are those whom I impressed deeply. They are neither the dead relatives nor God but real persons who are alive. I am not really alone even nobody around me because in my mind I have my friends, my family, they are there somehow. So sometimes I have internal communication with them no matter they are there or they are not there. I know what they would say, how they would react to me. Sometimes I know that they are smiling because I know they would make fun about it. Sometimes I think that they are interested in what I am doing because they want to learn from me. Sometimes I feel that they are watching me working because they want to see if I am lazy."

Example 86: This is an example of those who believe that God is watching them. "I believe in God. There is a personal relationship between God and me. God is a controller, and has power, and sees everything, and he is nice to us. It is good for our behaviour. Our mind is weakened. If we realize that we are watched by God, we will behave differently. For example, we see something very attractive, our mind wants to have it and saying: take it, take it! If we see that God is watching us, then you may suddenly know that your soul is saying: we actually do not need it. We should not take it. (Ask: is there somebody else besides God?) If somebody is there, so he or she is watching me. But they are not so important for me."

Example 87: This is another example of those who think that God is watching them. "If you do not concentrate, you will not know who is watching you because you go off into wild flights of fancy. (Ask: how do you feel?) I feel that, in fact, God is not watching you, he is examining you. If you examine yourself, you will find in your heart that something is watching you. (Ask: do you have this kind of feeling?) Yes. No matter what I do, I cannot cheat myself. For example, I tell a lie then my face will be flushed. I find in my heart that I am cheating. (Ask: has it something to do with people or God watching you or examining you?) Yes. In some religion, people give the examination power to God. They feel that God is examining them. I think that it is similar to what I said. When you are examining yourself, you feel that God is examining you. It means that the heart of God becomes the heart of yourself."

Example 88: This is an example of those who think that nobody watches them. "I do not think that someone watches me. I just do what I need to do. I feel free and unrestrained. I do everything by my conscience, in German "Gewissen". I think that I know what is right and what is wrong, what I should do and what I should not do. Even if someone watches me, I do not care. If I think that there is somebody watching me, talking to me, giving me direction, but the person is not there, I should go to see a doctor."

7.2 Whom You Pay Attention

The interview results about the question to whom you pay attention when you do something can be categorized into three kinds. The first is to pay attention to one's own experience. Some of them want to develop their free will, to persist in their own ways no matter what others say. Some of them want to follow the law of God, they believe that follow that guide, will have a good life. The second is to pay attention to others evaluation. They think that everybody is a member of society. If you want to be accepted by the society and by other people, you have to pay attention to others' evaluation. The third is to pay attention to both self experience and others' evaluation. They think that sometimes they do something which does not relate to others, for example, eating, or sleeping, they pay attention to their own experiences. Sometimes they do something which relates to others, for example, working, they must pay attention to others' evaluation. Sometimes they do something which seems have nothing to do with others but others may make a judgement though they may not speak it out. So both being accepted by others and being self enjoyable are important. For example, a dress which somebody myself enjoys but others dislike, wear it or not? (See Table 40 and Example 89-92)

Table 40: What You Pay Attention

	German Religious	German non Religious	Chinese Religious	Chinese non Religious	Total
Experience	3	1	3	1	8
Evaluation	1	4	3	0	8
Both	4	4	2	6	16

To compare the answers of the four groups, there are not many differences. Every opinion can be found in each group. Only a few people said something relating to religion. One is that they pay more attention to their own experience because they follow the law of God. The other is that they pay more attention to others' evaluation because they want to behave like a religious person.

Example 89: This is an example of those who pay attention to one's own experience. "I pay more attention to my experience and do what I want to do. In the past, I paid too much attention to others evaluation. Now I want to change it and to develop an independent personality. (Ask: why do you say that it is a wrong way?) This is a process. I realized that I was too dependent on others' evaluation in the past. In school, I was too concerned about other people, how do they think about me. It is a wrong way if you only want to fulfil others' expectations. It is a difficult task to get rid of others' manipulation. (Ask: why do you want to change?) Life is changeable. If I could become a free will person, have a free mind, I will be a happy person. I want to achieve it, self development."

Example 90: This is another example of those who pay attention to one's own experience. "Getting older, I am influenced more by my own experience. I do not care much about other's influence and other's opinions. The law of God guide me. If I follow, I will have a good life. (Ask: Is God similar to other people or different?) Quite different. Everybody has something bad but it is not possible for God."

Example 91: This is an example of those who pay attention to others evaluation. "I pay too much attention about what other people think about me. Do they respect me? My glory? My fame? Many actions are depended on this thinking. For example, being a religious person, I should have religious practice, to pray though sometimes I may spend the time do something else, to meditation though sometimes I may have other taste. What I do is because I know that other people evaluate me. It is very difficult to achieve it."

Example 92: This is an example of those who pay attention to both self experience and others′ evaluation. "I think that I must response to what I am doing. I must do things which I can stand for. I must be sure that I really want to do that. Of course, I do not live in an island, I am not alone, I need to look at others, to look at how they react to me. Is it acceptable by the people around me? Sometimes I may not do things which you want to do if others around you would not accept it. Sometimes I may just do it even if others do not accept it. It just depends."

7.3 Small Summary

To summarize the results: (1) Who is watching you? If you are not on stage facing some audiences, then to feel that someone is watching you is a psychological feeling. Some people feel that it is a real person who is watching them because ghosts or God never exists. Some people feel that it is God who is watching them because God is more important than others. Some people said that no matter a person or a god, all of them can become a conscience in your heart. It is your own heart examining yourself. (2) What you pay attention to? Some people said that they pay attention to their own experience. Some people said that they pay attention to others evaluation. Where is God? What is the interaction between people and God? Some who pay attention to their own experience said that they believe in their own experience because they follow the law of God. The law of God is absolutely right. God is their director. Some who pay attention to others evaluation also said that they listen to God because God sees everything. Some intentions which one should not have or behaviour which one should not do can be adjusted by the help of God.

8. The Concept of Religion

The last few questions of the interview are: "Do you think that you are a religious person or a non religious person?" "How do you distinguish yourself from others?" "How did you become a religious person or a non religious person?" "Do you think that you may become a non religious person from a religious person in the future or you may become a religious person from a non religious person in the future?" The first question is aimed to know people's self identity of being a religious person or a non religious person. The second question is aimed to find out people's concept of being religious or non religious. The third question is aimed to understand people's experience of being a religious person or a non religious person. The forth question is aimed to see the tendencies in their believe development.

8.1 Religious Person and Non Religious Person

The interview results about the question "Do you think that you are a religious person or a non religious person" show that there are three possibilities: One is to say yes. Two is to say no. Three is either to say yes but they think that their religious belief is different from others on some points or to say no but they express that they prefer observe the moral aspects of religious principles (See Example 93-94).

Example 93: This is an example of those who said that they are religious people but who think that their religious belief is different from others on some points. "I am a religious person but not in the way we see in the church. I do believe in God, Allah, Buddha, and so on, all of them are the same. There is one superior. I do not believe much in the Bible because it is written by man and they have their own ideas. I do not believe in church because I do not think a church has something to do with God. I think I am a religious person but only on the aspect that I have relationship with God. There is nothing in between."

Example 94: This is an example of those who do not think that they are very religious but they prefer to observe moral aspects of religious principles. "Maybe I am a little bit religious. Maybe you are surprised because I cannot think about life after death or the meaning of that. But I think religion is also related to the life now. It relates to how people can live with each other in peace or how people help others without getting anything back. (Ask: do you think that it is because religion influences you or social values influence you?) I think that religion influences me. I heard something on religion in school and in church when I was a child. I went to church when I was a child. Now I realized that those I heard in church are also social norms. I cannot really separate the social norms from religion. Apart from life after death, some norms you hear from the Christian religion are also social norms for people to live together. (Ask: what is the key point for being religious?) Maybe a religious person accepts a lot of things which you cannot explain. You just believe it but you cannot prove it in a concrete way. (Ask: do you think that someday you may become a religious person?) Maybe. I would not say that I think so but who knows."

The interview results for the question "How do you distinguish yourself from others as a religious person or a non religious person", according to the phrases which the interviewees used, can be categorized into two parts. One part is belief, for example, to believe in God, to believe in life after death, to believe in spirit, to believe in Karma; Another part is behaviour, for example, to observe religious norms, to go to the church, to practice meditation, to observe religious taboo (See Table 41 and Example 95-97). To compare what people said with what the scholar studied, not so many people talked about their religious experience from a micro view or religious organizations from a macro view.

Table 41: Concept of Religion

	German Religious	German non Religious	Chinese Religious	Chinese non Religious	Total
Spiritual	4	4	0	0	8
God	5	7	6	6	24
Eternal Life	3	7	0	1	11
Karma	2	0	2	0	4
Religious Norm	2	2	1	2	7
To Church	1	6	2	1	10
Taboo	1	0	0	1	2
Meditation	1	0	0	1	2

Example 95: This is an example of those who think that being a religious person they believe in God and life after death. "I try to be a religious person. The word religion comes from Latin, means to reconnect. To be a religious person means to have the desire to get connection with God. To be a religious man means to have relationship with God. In that sense, I can say that I am a religious man because I have a strong desire to have relationship with God. Actually I have not achieved very much. I am a beginner."

"I had some questions and I want to be answered when I was a child. I always think what happens after death. Then I was very sure that my life will continue after death when I was a young boy. This leads to a question what exactly happens after death? It does not make much sense that our life is limited, suddenly we go to the grave. I look for the answers. I read some philosophy books when I was a little bit older. The Christian scriptures impressed me much. Of course, I also think about what is my duty in this earth, what is my purpose in this life. Jesus answered my question in his teaching: You love God with all your heart. You love your neighbours with all your heart. Then my questions are how can I develop my love to God, my love to mankind? I have many things in my heart which are not nice. I envy often, am angry often, sometimes be lusty. All those things are natural but they keep me apart from the universal love. How can I overcome them? Then I found out in the Indian teaching the path to get this universal love. It gives us a clear way to develop our own loving, re-establish connection with God. That is why I decided to do this as my main purpose in life."

Example 96: This is an example of those who think that being a religious person they take God as an example, to cultivate one's moral character. "I believe in Buddha. Religion is a kind of belief, a belief of worship, a worship of God, or a worship of a being with super power. Buddhism is not a religion of worship which is different from other religion. (Ask: what is Buddha?) Buddha is an awakened person. He does not create anything and does not destroy anything. Philosophy is a science of seeking for the truth. Buddhism seeks for the truth but is not a science. (Ask: when you pray before the Buddha, what do you think?) I do not know what I think. I will not imagine things if I know what I think. I am just on the level of worship. (Ask: what is the statue of Buddha?) It is the symbol of our teacher, our model. It is Guanyin Buddha. Mao Zedong called us to learn from Leifeng (Leifeng is an example of servicing people), Buddha calls us to learn from Guanyin. The small book in my hand is an ode."

(Ask: How did you begin to believe in Buddha?) I always think that Buddhism is the most profound knowledge. I started to study it many years ago. I also think that Buddhism can help people solve problems. If we use the eyes of Buddhism to see many difficulties and troubles, the difficulties and troubles will not be the difficulties and troubles at all. I do not know how Christianity teaches people dealing with problems. Can Christianity teach people to change bad things into good things or to regard bad things as a punishment which one deserves?"

Example 97: This is an example of those who do not have religious beliefs. They have concepts of religion but they have their own opinions about religion. "I am not a religious person. I think that it has something to do with my scientific accomplishment because my profession requires me to be objective, to look at the world objectively. I see everything from the view of atheism. I think that my values and behaviour might be completely different from those who are religious. Religion, in my view, is a preconceived view. If I look at everything with this kind of view, everything will be different. Scientific education is to educate people to think independently, to judge independently. If one refers everything to God, he will never have the thoughts of his own."

8.2 Becoming Religious or Non Religious

The interview results about the question "How did you become a religious person or a non religious person" show that they became religious by reading books, thinking a lot, school education, the teaching of parents, participating in activities, cultural influence. In general, they are internal factors and external factors. Some people who are not religious originally become religious. Some people who are religious originally changed their religious beliefs. The former kind, for example, some Chinese people who were educated by the Marxist materialism when they were in China, then became religious persons after they came to Germany because of the change of the cultural environment. The latter kind, for example, some German people who were influenced much by their religious tradition when they were very young, then changed their religious beliefs when they grew up because they thought independently and made their own decisions (See Table 42 and Example 98-99).

Table 42: How Develop the Concepts

	German Religious	German non Religious	Chinese Religious	Chinese non Religious	Total
Reading	2	0	3	0	5
Thinking	4	8	0	4	16
Parents	0	4	1	0	5
School	2	0	0	7	9
Group	3	0	6	0	9
Culture	1	0	6	1	8

Example 98: This is an example of those who are not religious originally then become religious. "I tend to believe in Christianity but I am not a Christian yet. I think that it is better to have religious beliefs than to have not religious beliefs. Belief is something which is not written in law but can bind people's behaviour. Some beliefs seem good but they are too concrete and are difficult to achieve. It makes people feel disappointed. It will be vanished in people's mind. I began to know Christianity after I came to Germany. I go to church often and I obtained knowledge there. I think that Christianity has great impact. It has its own organization, its own way of practicing, its own force. If someone believes in it, he will think of what he does should conform what the God likes. Otherwise he will be punished. If everybody recognizes this, the whole society will be stable."

Example 99: This is an example of those who are religious originally then they changed their religious beliefs. "I was a Roman Catholic in the past because my father and mother educated me that. It was just six months ago, I decided to leave the church because I could not understand its position, attitude, and so on. A few month ago, when I ate at the church the last time, I thought, why I ate at church? I thought about it for a year already. I paid a lot of church tax, why? I doubt it is useful there. I may spend the money for other things."

(Ask: what did your parents think about your leaving?) "I did not talk about it to my parents. I do not think that it has too much problems for them. My mother is in another church. I have to assist her or the three of us together to a priest. I think that you are dependant when you are small. It is not too surprising. Since the church plays the role at practical life, it is also not surprising that a lot of people question their attitude and think about leaving there. (Ask: what role did the church play in the past?) I do not know. I think it gives less moral teaching to the people now. It should be very much dominate in everyday life. I think that the whole culture based on the society. Some are still determined by their influence of church, a lot of ethical, moral principles are still alive but it is no longer obvious connecting with the original source.

Chapter 6: Discussion and Conclusion

1. Relationship between People and Immortals

The word immortal means living forever. It can be used to describe something living forever, for example, immortal life. It can also be used to refer somebody living forever, for example, immortal God. In this research, the two meanings are included. For example: Life after death contains the meaning of something living forever, for instance, soul living forever; Ancestor worship contains the meaning of somebody living forever, for instance, the dead relatives living forever. The relationship between people and immortals can be explained as the relationship between this life and the next life of one person, can also be explained as the relationship between the living people and the dead people. God, is a supernatural being. He is regarded by the religious people as an immortal. If someone believes in God, he also believes that God can give his character of immortality to human beings.

The word immortal is also used by the people who do not have religious beliefs. It can be used to describe something living forever, for example, the immortal deeds. It means that the deeds will never be obliterated. It can be used to refer somebody living for ever, for example, the immortal heroes. It means that the heroes will be eternal glory. If someone says that something passed but it seems that it still exists, it means that something leaves an indelible impression. If someone says that somebody died but it seems that he is still living, it means that people cherish the memory of somebody. When the Chinese people mourn over a person's death, they would say: Comrade So and So, Eternal Glory! Rest in Peace! In the following sections, the relationship between the people and the immortals from the view of the people who accepted the investigation will be discussed.

1.1 Intrapersonal Relationship between People and Immortals

The intrapersonal relationship between people and immortals refers to the relationship between the one in this life (the living self) and the one after death (the dead self). From the view of the people who have religious beliefs, there is a relationship between the living self in this world and the dead self in the hereafter. This relationship is spiritual not physical. The soul from the view of western religion, for example, Christianity, or the action from the view of eastern religion, for example, Buddhism, makes the two selves connected. A pure soul or good action in this world will lead people to a happy life in next world. A dirty soul or bad action in this world will lead people to a miserable life in the next world. What does a happy life or a miserable life look like? Few people can answer it concretely. They say that it will be in another place (in heaven, on earth, or under the ground) and another form (still like the human life now or like an animal's life possibly).

For example, one of the interviewees talked about life after death: "Death of my body means that I will no longer have something to do with this world. When I appear again in another form of life, even if I can return to this world, the world is not the original face from my eyes. The relationship between the world and I will be changed as well. (Ask: what kind of world from your eyes? what kind of relationship?) I may become a dog hereafter. The world from a pair of eyes of a dog will certainly be different from the world from a pair of eyes of a man. Of course, the relationship will be changed along with the changes of eyes." This example means that the life of the living self has something to do with the life of the dead self but once he goes to another world, the person of the new self will have nothing to do with the person of the old self.

From the view of the people who do not have religious beliefs, there is no relationship between the living self today and the dead self hereafter. Everybody has only one life in this world. Any spiritual things, for example, soul, cannot be functioning without a functioning brain. Everybody stops his action when his body physically dies. Nobody knows about himself and the public judgement about his right and wrong after he dies. But they believe that good will be rewarded with good and evil with evil. Good ones will be praised and bad ones will be cursed by later generation.

One example of this is: "I just have one life. The life will continue until my body is dead. But I think that there is a relationship between what I do now and hereafter. I do not know why I have the feeling that some people died, they do not exist anymore, but they left their foot print on the earth. I often think: how good it will be if I can do something worthwhile in my limited life, leave my foot print on the earth. If it is so, I will have a feeling of making achievement. It is pity that I may not reach the goal. Of course, I will make effort." This example means that nobody can avoid death no matter how he behaves when he is alive. Death is the same for everybody. But the foot print which one leaves to the later generation may always be associated with one's name. The Chinese former chairman Mao Zedong wrote in his work "Commemorate Zhang Side" (an ordinary man who died at his post): "Though death befalls all man alike, it may be weightier than a mountain or lighter than a feather." To weigh up the weight of a mountain and a feather, the value of one's life is measured.

The following figure illustrates the different perspectives of the people who have religious beliefs and who do not have religious beliefs on intrapersonal relationships between people and immortals. The first one describes the intrapersonal relationship from the view of the religious people. The second one describes the intrapersonal relationship from the view of the non religious people (See Figure 9).

Figure 9: Intrapersonal Relationship Between People and Immortals

From the View of the Religious People

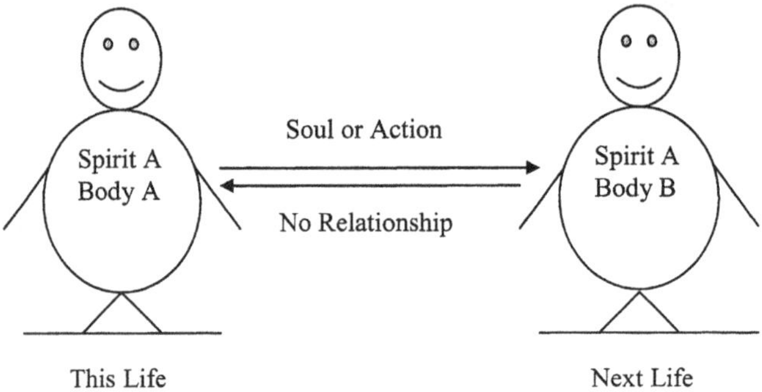

From the View of the Non Religious People

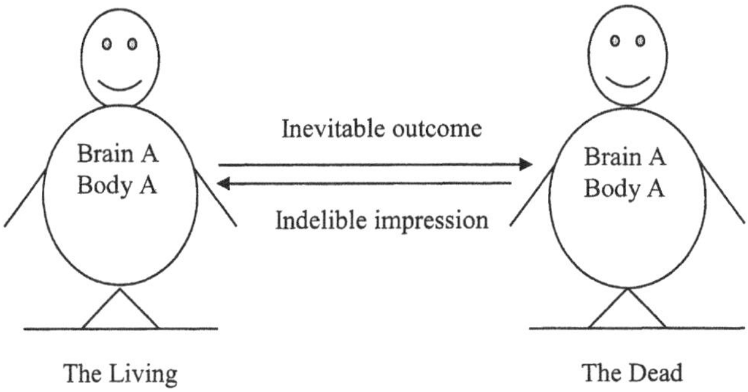

1.2 Interpersonal Relationship between People and Immortals

Interpersonal relationship between people and immortals refers to the relationship between the living people and the immortal others. The immortal others include dead relatives, ancestors, God, and people themselves after they die relating to their descendants. From the view of the people who have religious beliefs, their dead relatives are still living somewhere, in the place where their soul or action led them to. People can contact them but only when their heart is there. The relationship between the living people and their dead relatives changes or finishes after the relatives die but the contact between the living people and their dead relatives may continue. Ancestors are still living somewhere, just like their dead relatives. It is supposed in the dissertation that people may regard their ancestors as supernatural beings and worship them. But this concept can only be found among the Chinese religious people, not among the German religious people. Even if among the Chinese religious people, it is not a very representative viewpoint in this investigation though it might be still popular in China, especially in the vast rural areas. God is an immortal charismatic being from the view of the people who sincerely believe in it. He is a moral model and a fair judge in the religious believers' heart. He is also a life consulter and director of the religious people. God is a creator who created everybody and everything. The relationship between people and God is permanent. The contact between people and God is permanent. Descendants, some people think that God created man, including they themselves and their descendants. All of them are equal before God. Each of them is an independent individual concerning the relationship with God. The relationship between people and their descendants will change or finish after they die but the contact between the people and their descendants will continue.

From the view of the people who do not have religious beliefs, their dead relatives died forever, like they themselves will die. The dead relatives will never be alive again. They can only live in their memory. They have permanent relationship with their dead relatives because of the blood ties but they can no longer have contact with them. Their ancestors died forever as well, like their dead relatives. But what the ancestors created when they are alive, for example, the human culture in a broad sense, or the family property in a narrow sense, is handed down from their time. People respect them and worship them. God is an unreal being created in some people's mind. It is impossible that God has power over humans. He never is involved in human affairs. Humans never and will not have any relationship or contact with God. Descendants are given birth by their parents. The older generation is the origin of the younger generation. The younger generation is lifeblood of the older generation. The blood ties always exist. They have permanent relationship with each other but they cannot contact each other after the people they themselves die.

The following figure illustrates the different perspectives of the people who have religious beliefs and who do not have religious beliefs on the interpersonal relationships between people and the immortals. The first one describes the interpersonal relationship from the view of the religious people. The second one describes the interpersonal relationship from the view of the non religious people (See Figure 10).

1.3 Integration of the Concepts of Immortals

In the theoretical part of the dissertation, the concept of religious beliefs was introduced. They are divided into two aspects: the beliefs in the spirit and the beliefs in God. The investigation results in this research show that these two aspects are not separate but relate to each other. To repeat the words from an interview, the relationship between the spirit of humans and God is: "Man is created by God. It is God who placed his spirit in man's heart. He used mud moulding man's body. Because there is a spirit of God in man's body, man can present their vivid lifelike. The life of a body is limited while the spirit is eternal."

Figure 10: Interpersonal Relationship between People and Immortals

From the View of the Religious People

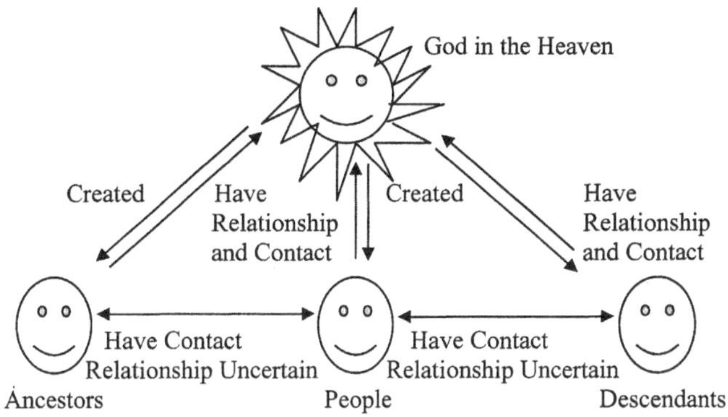

From the View of the Non Religious People

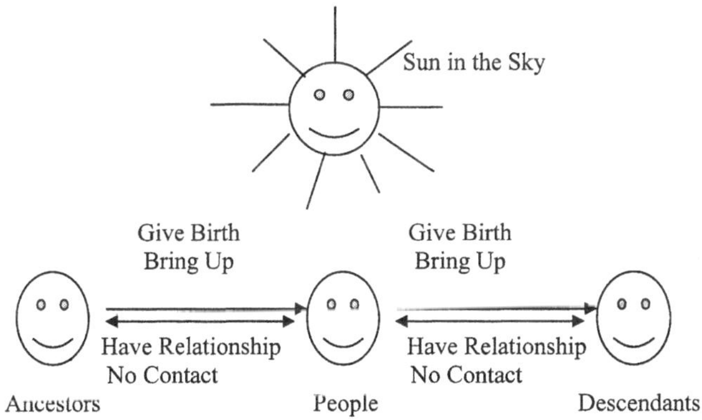

There is a common belief among all the religious people that something spiritual is eternal. From the view of western religion, for example, Christianity, this eternal thing is the soul. From the view of eastern religion, for example, Buddhism, this eternal thing is action. The soul can guide people to another life hereafter, heaven or hell, which is called retribution. Action can drive people to another level, higher or lower, which is called Karma. These beliefs are introduced in the theoretical part. These are agreed by the religious people in this research as well. God is a supernatural being which is believed in by all the religious people. From the view of western religion, for example, Christianity, God is a charismatic and powerful leader of humans. From the view of eastern religion, for example, Buddhism, God is a noble and prestigious model of humans. The western God created humans. He always stands high above humans. While the eastern God stands high above humans as well but everybody might reach that level by making effort (See Figure 11).

Comparative religious study is not the focal point of this dissertation but it is interesting to find from previous research and this research the different concepts of religion among the religious believers. It is also important to have this knowledge for the future studies, for example, to study the influence of different religious beliefs on social interaction. Beside the different beliefs in God from the view of western religion and eastern religion, the different beliefs in ancestors from the view of the German people and the Chinese people is another issue which is worth discussing.

Ancestor worship is a Chinese tradition which has a long history. For the ordinary people, ancestor worship resulted from secular feelings of love for the dead relatives. The worship for the soul of a deceased person, the contact between the living people and their ancestors' spirit becomes an important consciousness of religion. The expressions of this consciousness are: The first is to be grateful to the ancestors because the ancestors created a splendid national culture for the descendants. The second is to pray to the ancestors for the protection because the soul of the ancestors can protect the descendants. The third is to show filial piety to the ancestors because the descendants have a permanent relationship with their ancestors, they are the continuity of the life of the ancestors', having descendants around, people will not be lonely after they die (Hou Jie and Fan Lizhu 1994: pp. 230-259).

Figure 11: Western God and Eastern God

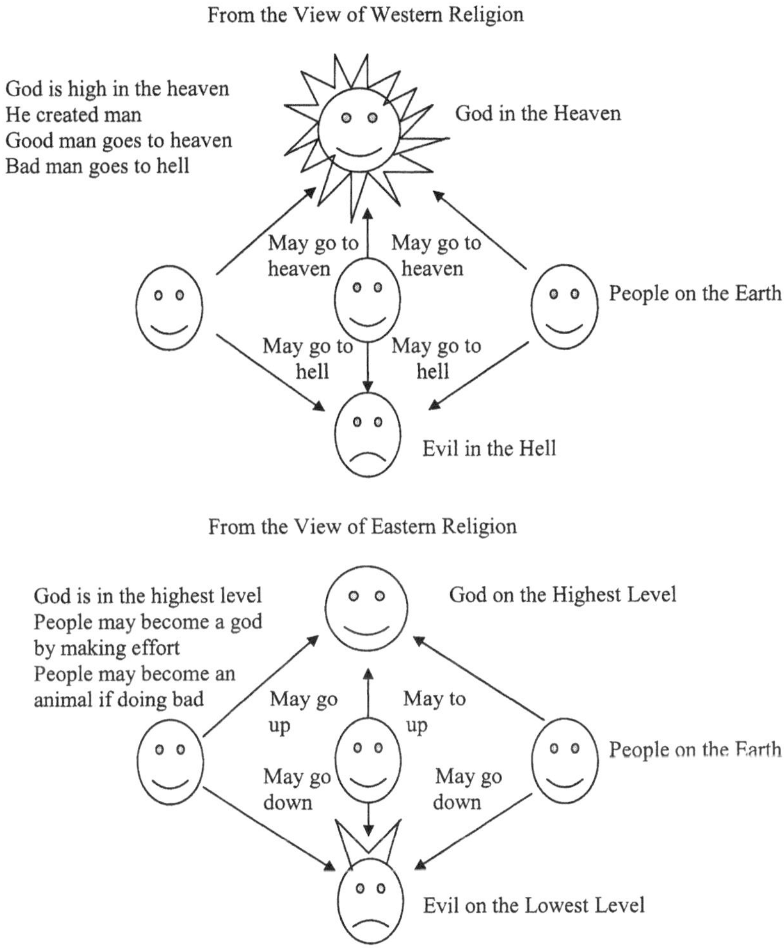

The implications of ancestor worship or the contents of it can be summarized in four Chinese characters: Shen Zhong Zhui Yuan (in Chinese 慎终追远). Shen Zhong means to deal with funeral for the older generation according to certain rite. Zhui Yuan means to offer sacrifices for the ancestors to memorize the source of life. The objects of the worship may be the ancestors' high personality and great achievements. It may not have a very strong concept of blood relationship but have a great deal of cultural value. The objects of worship may also be the older generation, father or grandfather. The purpose of doing it is to strengthen the blood relationship of the family, to inherit and develop the achievements of the ancestors, to allow the family to continue developing (Mu Zhongjian 2000: pp. 47-57).

To compare the concept of ancestors of the Chinese people with the concept of God of the western people, the western people think that ancestors and God are different. To review the results from the interview, the differences are: Ancestors did live in this world and gave birth to the descendants. Ancestors and descendants have a blood relationship. God might or might not live in this world according to different beliefs but he created human beings including the ancestors as well. God and human beings have spiritual relationship. From the view of western people, ancestors are humans, they do not have the nature of God. However, Chinese people have the concept of both the supernatural God and the immortal ancestors. The results from the interview show that the two concepts are expressed by Chinese people. They are nurtured in the Chinese culture but many of them accepted western religious thoughts after they go abroad. In China, especially in the vast rural area of China, ancestor worship can be presented in everyday life. Another kind of religious atmosphere which differs from the Chinese religious society in Munich might be experienced.

2. Interaction between People and Immortals

The discussion above illustrated the similarities and the differences of the relationship between people and immortals. People who have religious beliefs and who do not have religious beliefs have different relationships with immortals. Even those who have similar religious beliefs are influenced by their cultural environment more or less. The investigation results show that these differences and influences are reflected in the social interaction of the people as well.

2.1 Interaction with Strangers

To review the investigation results about the interaction with strangers, getting close to others no matter in the situation of being a stranger in a strange place or treating a stranger in a familiar place is the representative behaviour, though some people take more initiative while some people are relatively passive, some people are more open while some people are comparatively cautious. Some people who take initiative when being a stranger seem relatively passive when seeing a stranger. Some people who are relatively passive when being a stranger become initiative when seeing a stranger. The former ones take initiative first then become passive because of their own needs. The latter ones are passive first then take initiative because of their introversion character.

Though the behaviours of the most people are similar, the investigation results show that the motives of getting close to others are different. To win the honour of God is one of the motives which is expressed by the people who believe in God. To fulfill the needs of people is another one of the motives which is expressed from most people regardless what they believe. To be gregarious so as not to be lonely is the third kind of answers which is expressed from the people who cannot bear loneliness. The word “need” was used more often than the others. It can be explained from the result of the research that interaction with strangers itself is one of the human needs on the one hand and humans have to interact with strangers in order to fulfil their varied needs on the other hand.

It is supposed that people who have religious beliefs and people who do not have religious beliefs may have something different in the interaction with strangers. It turned out that there are not many differences in the behaviour. There are some differences in the motives, however, it is not everybody who believes in God associates their interaction with God. Somebody raised a question in a Bible study meeting in the Biblekreis (a Chinese Christian society in Munich): When you do something good, do you want to win the honour of God or do you want to win favour of God? It derives a further question: What is the position of God and of Self in one's heart? From the view of social psychology, a need is a reflection in the individuals' mind when they feel something lacking in life. Motive is a force which impels individuals to fulfil the need. The way that the individuals try to fulfil the need is behaviour. Behaviour is visible while the motive is invisible but the two are interrelated. Need is the root cause of initiative and motive is the direct reason of behaviour. An individual has many needs and motives. According to their effect, they can be categorized into the primary and the secondary. The primary motive is dominative. Motives may emerge and change over time. It is an expression of individuals' thoughts, beliefs and morals. The results of this research show that there are many motives behind the interaction. The question is what is the primary motive of them? The goal of the behaviour is God, or self, or others (Shen Decan 1995: pp. 63-75)?

One sentence that is repeated by a certain number of people when talking about interactions with strangers is: "It depends". In the situation of being a stranger in strange place, they distinguish different groups: to have working contact with colleagues naturally, to share the same interests with fellows in a club happily, and to talk with people in a cafeteria carefully. They distinguish different individuals: they prefer to get close to those who are friendly and helpful. Even in a specific situation, they still need to think in detail. For example, when others offer a help, they will see: What are their motives, do they want to help me? What are their attitudes, do they treat me warmly? In the situation of treating a stranger in a familiar place, they also consider themselves and the opposite side: How much am I interested? How much does he need? In a specific situation, for example, others make a suggestion, they will see: Is it reasonable? Is he experienced? All those show that the interaction between people is a complex process: sending words and cues and receiving and processing words and cues as they come in from the other side. It is just likes what is introduced in the theoretical part of the dissertation that people negotiate which roles they are going to play in a situation. For example: when they need help, they emit cues to others by getting close to others, when others make a suggestion on their work, they verify others conformity by asking if he is experienced.

In the section of interaction with strangers, there is a special topic to explain why a man and a women fall in love at first sight or divorce after living together for many years and why two persons feel like old friends at first meeting or know each other for a long time but fight often. Some people explain that it is because of fate. Some people explain that it is because of other reasons. It is supposed that fate is the explanation of the people who have religious beliefs. It is true that some religious believers explained it this way. Results from the interview explained it in detail. The alternative words for fate which people used are Karma and Yuanfen. The normal definitions of fate, Karma and Yuanfen are: Fate is power that cannot be resisted that determines something destined to happen. Karma is action of one's previous life regarded as deciding his fate for the future life. Yuanfen is chance or good luck decided by fate by which people are brought together. It mentioned in the preceding chapter that the three terms are not completely the same. Fate stresses destiny. Karma stresses cause and effect. Yuanfen stresses chance or luck. But people use them interchangeably.

Most people explain that it is because of other reasons which are different from the explanations of power, action, or chance befalling from a sacred cosmos but existing in everyday life. To fall in love at first sight is because of attraction that makes people interested in each other, because of emotion that arouses men and women an enthusiasm, because of congruence that ideal person in mind appears before eyes. To divorce after living together for many years is because the foundation of the marriage is not solid, because something changed after the marriage among the two persons, because they neglected to cultivate the relationship after marriage, because a third person pushed into a queue out of turn. To feel like friends at first meeting is because of the similarities between the two persons. To fight each other often for a long time is because of the differences between the two persons. Falling in love or making friends are very traditional topics which researchers have studied in many fields. Those traditional topics are discussed again in this dissertation, it is not for exploring the reasons that people falling in love or making friends but for exploring the views that people have it in order to see if there are differences among the people who have different beliefs.

Some people made comments on the statements. It is possible to fall in love at first sight but this love is not reliable. It seems that two people attract each other but they may be incompatible in fact. It is hard to say that if it is a love of everlasting or it is a flash in the pan. Feelings are built up by interactions between the two persons. It is impossible to feel that strangers are like old friends at first meeting because most who become friends experienced over a period of time, many times of meet, many times contact. How can people be friends without understanding?

These two questions relate to explaining some certain phenomena rather than describing normal behaviour. So the differences between the people who have religious beliefs and who do not have religious beliefs are expressed. Those who have religious beliefs explain certain phenomena befalling from a sacred cosmos. Those who do not have religious beliefs explain certain phenomena existing in actual life. How do their beliefs influence their behaviour, their interaction with lovers and friends? If people believe that there is a power befalling from a sacred cosmos which they cannot master, it means that everything is arranged by fate, they are controlled by fate not by themselves, how do they face life, for example, love or divorce, find friends or meet enemies? They may take it for granted when they have lovers or friends even if the opposite side are not true. They may not want to improve a bad relationship when they find enemy even if the situation can be possibly changed. If people believe that all the influential factors exist in actual life are created by people themselves, it means that everything depends on man's effort, they themselves determine their fate, how do they face life, for example, love or divorce, find friends or meet enemies? They may think that everything is possible and changeable. It is possible for everything to emerge and to vanish. They are more realistic. As to what people do in reality, it needs to be studied more in the future.

2.2 Interaction with Intimates

To review the investigation results about the interaction with intimates, the results from the questionnaire show that most people gave a positive answer about the interaction with their intimates: to lay bare thoughts to their intimates, to express feelings to their intimates, to share interests with their intimates, and to understand each other. People of the four groups are similar on some aspects and different on some other aspects. The differences are not reflected between the religious people and the non religious people but reflected between the German people and the Chinese people. Both the Germans and the Chinese pay attention mostly to understanding each other in their interactions while the

Germans rate the disclosure of thoughts as the second important aspect and the Chinese put the sharing feelings as the second important aspect. Interaction between intimates is seemed intimate. The relationship between intimates should be harmonious. But in reality inharmonious phenomena between the intimates are a common occurrence. How can this be explained?

The people who gave other answers are small in number. Their answers have a common character which can be expressed by their own words "In between". That means their answers are between the two given answers one and two. If the two given answers are the two points of a scale, their answers are in a certain point between the two extreme points. It shows a principle in the process of social interaction, a principle of appropriateness. Otherwise things may run counter to one's desire, they said. In philosophy, there is a principle, the virtue of mean. A man should have an ability to control his behaviour, not to go to the extremes. When we deal with something, we should deal with it not to go too far to control, not to go too near to reach the goal. An open question is: In what situation do people behave as much as one likes heartily or enjoy oneself thoroughly?

The results from the interview show as well that most people would like to share behaviour with their intimates and to share experience with their intimates. But on each of the aspects, there are some people who raised their own questions. When the interview question is about to lay bare thoughts to the intimates, they asked: whom to lay bare, partner or parents? When the interview question is about to express feelings to the intimate, they asked: what kind of feelings, happy or angry? When the interview question is about to share interests with the intimates, they asked: how to share, really to do or just look? When the interview question is about to understand each other, they said: I always try it but I am not sure. It is as same as the answer about interaction with strangers that "it depends" is a typical answer. It similar to what is introduced in the theoretical part that people negotiate which roles they are going to play in a situation. For example: when they interact with their intimates, regardless if it involves sharing behaviour or experience, they constantly inform each other about themselves in order to identify themselves.

In the section of interaction with intimates, there is a special topic to investigate why parents bring up children and if it is important for one to have children, why parents have many expectations of children and if it is meaningful for parents themselves. The investigation results show that some people associate children with something sacred, most people associate children with their actual life. It is supposed that people who have religious beliefs may associate children with something sacred. It turned out that only a few people expressed that way. To tell the reasons why parents bring up children and why parents have many expectations of children, some people said: Children are the gifts of God, God is happy to see it. It is a decree of God. In this sense, bringing up children is important and meaningful. Some people have a different opinion. Still associate something sacred, some people do not think that it is important and meaningful. They said that many people want to have children because they seek for love relationship with children. Instead of having a love relationship with children, they want to develop love relationship with God. They said that many people hope to extend their life by having children but they believe that their life will be extended because their mind will be reincarnated.

From the perspectives of the people who do not have religious beliefs, the positive opinions of having children are to have one who belongs to them because children are their own properties or accessories, to fulfill their psychological needs because they seek for an intimate relationship with children, to provide for their aged because they hope children taking care of them, to do their duty for society because the society needs successors, or to spend a natural life because it is a human being's nature. The negative opinions of having children are to loose their own freedom because children occupy their time and energy, to be unnecessary to have children because they have nephews and nieces, to be bad increase the population because the population is already excessive, to be spin a cocoon around self because people have right to make their own choice to have or not to have children.

Some people, especially some Chinese people think that children are the extension of their life. Is it a religious concept? It could be and it could be not. From the view of having children in order to show filial piety to the ancestors, to continue the life of their ancestors also themselves otherwise they will be blamed to forfeit incense and candles burning at a temple also by their graves, it is religious because it contains the meaning of immortal ancestors living forever and immortal ancestors having successors. From the view of having children in order to have genes inherited or continue the cause of themselves, it is not religious because it contains the meaning of biological concept and the cause of the ancestors having successors.

Connecting the issue of the relationship between people and their ancestors and their descendants, the parents and children relationship can be categorized into two types in general: One is the relationship of a chain. The older generation has permanent connection with the younger generation even if they die; Two is the relationship of a relay. Everyone walks through one section of the whole human being's history. How do their beliefs influence their behaviour, the interactions with children or parents? The sources which young parents can offer to the children are two kinds: visible or material and invisible or spiritual. The visible or material source is, for example, money. The invisible or spiritual source is, for example, attitude. The visible money is something that you can touch. The invisible attitude is something that you can only sense. The parents and children relationship is not something that you can touch but a thing that you can sense with heart. Children can experience the meaning behind the money though they sometimes cannot express. Somebody asked: why do you bringing up children and have expectations of Children? In order to educate children? Or in order to compensate yourself? When the young parents become old and the children grow up, the old can get feedback from the youth. If the parents love their children, the children love them. If it seems that parents love children but doing everything for themselves in fact, what is the result? As you sow, so will you reap.

These two questions again relate to explaining a certain relationship rather than describing normal behaviour. So the differences between the people who have religious beliefs and who do not have religious beliefs are expressed. There are different opinions among the groups. Some people think that bringing up children and have high expectations of children is important and meaningful because children are the gifts of God and children is decreed by God from the view of the religious people, and because children can fulfill their needs and the society needs from the view of the non religious people. Some people think that it is not that important and meaningful because to develop a love relationship with God is more important than with children and their life will be continued which is nothing to do with children from the view of the religious people, and because to keep their own freedom is more important than to give it to children and to develop love relationship with relatives and friends is the same as with children from the view of the non religious people. Whatever does it mean from the perspective of the religious people? Are children important and meaningful for the parents or not? How do those beliefs influence people giving birth to children and bringing up children in everyday life? More studies are needed in the future.

2.3 Interaction with Immortals

In the theoretical part of the dissertation, some previous studies on religious experience are introduced. For example: It can be an experience of direct awareness or encounter with a divine being. It can also be an experience of the presence of a supernatural being. Religious believers may have this experience through a common, public, sensory object or may have this experience through an unusual, public, sensory object. Some of the experience can be described in normal sensible language and some of the experience cannot be described in normal sensible language. It is important to understand what people really experience. Do they really experience a supernatural reality or do they only interpret certain experiences religiously? In my research, religious experience is focused on the interaction between the people and immortals in the beyond.

There are legends in ancient China in which immortals descend to the man's world. The characteristics of immortals are that they are man like and long life. They are leisurely and magical. Where they descend, there the people live a life of plenty. There are idioms used in everyday life describing the immortals' magic. For example: Shen Chai Gui Shi (in Chinese 神差鬼使), means doings of ghosts and gods, unexpected happenings, a curious coincidence. Shen Chu Gui Mo (in Chinese 神出鬼没), means to come and go like ghosts and gods, something appears and disappears mysteriously. To review the investigation results about the interaction with immortals, two kinds of questions are raised. One is how people solve problems and attribute problems, pray the immortals for help or think of other ways, to attribute it to fate or other factors. Anothr is how do people feel and what people pay attention to when doing something, feel of being watchedby immortals or by other people, pay attention to self experience or others' evaluation.

Results from the people who have religious beliefs show that it is true that some religious people pray when they suffer setbacks. They tell God the truth sincerely and hope to get help from God earnestly. But the percentage of those people is low. Besides they pray, they also look for other ways to solve problems. They do attribute those problems to fate. They think that it is what one should deserve. But the percentage of those people is also low. Besides they attribute to fate, they also think about other factors. The results from the people who have religious beliefs show that they really feel to be watched by immortals or to be watched by immortals and other people. They feel the existence of God because they think that God is more important than others. What do they pay attention to? Some people pay attention to their own experience because what they follow the law of God. Some people pay attention to others' evaluation because they think that God is the most important other. What is the difference between the two kinds of people? The former internalised God in heart, the latter feel the God's power in a distance.

Results from the people who have not religious belief show that they always look for other ways to solve problems rather than pray. They analyse problems, examine errors, and ask for other ideas. They adjust themselves, change attitudes, shift attention. Sometimes they just accept it and forget about it. They attribute problems to internal factors, to see if they are wrong or if they have asked for the trouble. They attribute problems to external factors, to see if others cooperate or if the environment is favourable. They attribute problems to internal and external factors, alternative or simultaneous. The results from the people who do not have religious beliefs show that some people feel to be watched by other people though sometimes there are no people around at all. They feel there is a binding force from outside by the eyes of mass. Some people feel that nobody watches them. They are free and unrestrained. They do everything with conscience. Some people pay attention to their own experience because they want to develop free will. Some people pay attention to others' evaluation because they hope to be accepted by others. When does a person feel happy? Enjoy self or being accepted by others?

3. The Influence of Religious Beliefs on Social Interaction

In the first section of this chapter, it summarized different beliefs of the people, religious and non religious. It discussed the relationship of the living self and the dead self and how to view the relationship of the living self and the dead others. In the second section of this chapter, it reviewed the various interactions among the people who have religious beliefs and who do not have religious beliefs. In this section, it will discuss the influence of religious beliefs on social interaction. In the theoretical part of the dissertation, the relationship between religious beliefs and social interaction was introduced. A Chinese Qigong example was made which revealed the role of religious beliefs in the process of interaction. After a practical survey and careful analysis, a better understanding of it can be obtained: First, in what condition do beliefs take effect, Second, on what aspects do beliefs take effect. Third, how many roles do beliefs possibly play.

3.1 Condition that Beliefs Taking Effect

Examples from the religious believers illustrate that they can only interact with the dead relatives, ancestors, or God when their heart is there. Examples from the non religious believers illustrate that the dead relatives or ancestors can only be alive in their heart. What is heart? The heart is the centre of the emotions. There are many expressions which use the term heart to express people's emotions. For example: When we say we are grateful to the ancestors from our heart, which means we are grateful to the ancestors sincerely. When we say we love God with all our heart, which means we love God completely. Heart is the centre of beliefs taking effect. If somebody believes something without heart, the belief is only in word. To say yes and mean no or say one thing and mean another, it will not be efficacious. So the heart is the condition of beliefs taking effect. It is only possible that the immortals, the dead relatives, ancestors, or God, may present when the people's heart is there. If somebody says something with heart, the opposite side also listens attentively. If somebody says something without heart, the opposite side also listens carelessly (See Figure 12).

Figure 12: Interact with Immortals with Heart

Both the religious people and the non religious people associate themselves with the "immortals" with heart. What is the difference? For example, both a religious person and a non religious person feel that their dead relatives' word ringing in their ears and their dead relatives' smile appearing before their eyes. The religious person may interpret it as a reality while the non religious person will interpret it as a fantasy. Or both a religious person and a non religious person have a guilty conscience to their dead relatives. They know that their dead relatives must blame them according to the conventions and they really feel that their dead relatives do. The religious persons think that it is true while the non religious persons think that it is false though he should be blamed (See Figure 13).

Figure 13: Different Interpretation about the Dead

From the View of the Religious People

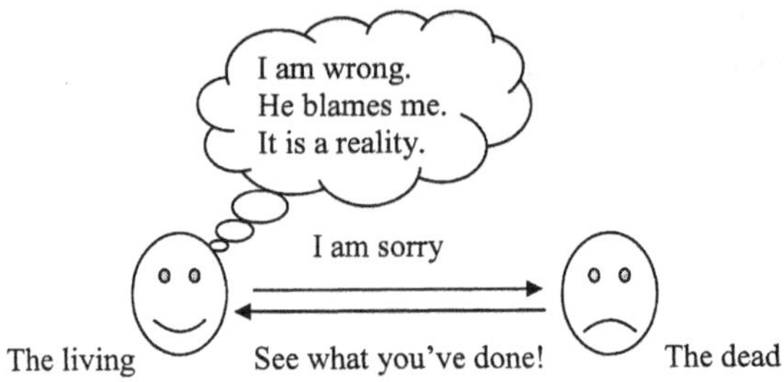

From the View of the Non Religious People

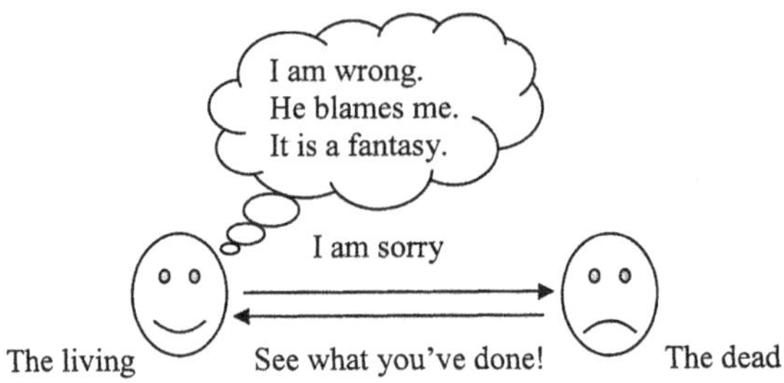

On each question, there are people who show their uncertainty, confusion, or contradiction. The typical expression of this is "I am not sure". For Example: When the question was about belief in death, they said: "I do not know because I am still alive and I have not the experience of death yet." (It is uncertain) Or "I know life will finish after death but I hope it continues, might be." (It is confusion) When the question was about life after death, they said: "I think about it but there is no hint to choose what is right and what is wrong." (It is uncertain) Or "Life should be limited until one's body dies from the view of natural science but what about after death? I do not what to think about it, it is a matter of a distant future" (It is confusion) When the question was about dead relatives, they said: "Of course I will die when my body dies. But I believe my dead relatives are in the heaven. I do not know what heaven looks like but my dead relatives have a happy life there." (It is contradiction)

How can the answers be explained? From the view of sociology, socialization is a long process, it is a normal phenomenon that somebody feels uncertainty, confusion or contradiction in mind sometimes during that long process. To "life cycle theory" of demograph, it can be explained that everyone experiences two processes in life, one is life cycle, from young to old, the other is social change, from one historical period to another. Life cycle is a natural series of events taking place to everyone. Social change is a crucial alternation taking place in society sometimes slowly sometimes rapidly. Social change may involve all fields: politics, economics, culture, and religion. It is possible that people's beliefs change along with the changes of life events and social history in the two processes. A world from an adult's eyes may seem different from a child's eyes. A world in this historical period may seem different from that historical period. When the old beliefs are wavering, the new beliefs have not built, the uncertainty, confusion or contradiction appears. Some people, for example, some Chinese people, they experience a social mobility, from one country to another country. This may also bring them a lot of changes as well. The question is: if a sincere and firm heart is the condition for beliefs to take effect, what will be the result of half-believing and half-doubting? What is the relationship between the development of religious beliefs and the development or changes of social environment?

3.2 Aspects that Beliefs Taking Effect

On the basis of the differences in social interactions between the people who have religious beliefs and who do not have religious beliefs, we can find that on what aspects the religious beliefs take effect.

- When asking people to describe their interaction with strangers, getting close to others is the representative answer. To fulfill the needs of people is expressed by most people regardless what they believe. To win the honour of God is one of the motives which can distinguish the religious people and the non religious people, but only a few who identify themselves as religious said. Some people said: it depends.

- When asking people to explain why some people love each other at first sight or some people divorce after living together for many years and why some people feel like old friends at first meeting and some people fight each other often though knowing for a long time, fate is one of the explanations by some religious people. Other reasons are the explanation of most non religious people.

- When asking people to describe their interaction with intimate, sharing behaviour and experience with intimates is the most identical answer. Understanding each other is the number one aspect which most people agree. To disclose thoughts to intimates is the second big group of people from the Germans and sharing feelings with the intimates is the second big group of people from the Chinese. It seems that there are not differences between the people who have religious beliefs and who do not have religious beliefs. Some people again said: it depends. Some people expressed in the way of appropriateness.

- When asking people to explain if it is important and meaningful for the parents to give birth and bring up children, some religious people associate the issues with something sacred but they have different opinions. Some of them think that it is important and meaningful because God decrees it. Some of them think that it is not important and meaningful because God is the most important being while children are not. Most people associate it with actual life but they also have different opinions. Some of them have positive attitude toward having children. Some of them have negative attitude toward having children.
- When asking people to tell how they solve problems and attribute problems, a small number of religious people said that they pray to the immortals for help. Most people think of other ways. A small number of religious people attribute problems to fate. Most people attribute it to other factors.
- When asking people who watch them and whom they pay attention to when they do something, some religious people said that God watches them. Most people think that other people watch them or nobody watches them. Some religious people pay attention to others' evaluation, this other is God. Some religious people pay attention to self experience because they follow the law of God. Most people pay attention to both others' evaluation and self experience.

What can be found from the above? More or less religious beliefs take effect on the aspects which is involved in the research. The investigation results show that when religious people describe their normal behaviour, for example, interaction with strangers and intimates, they associate with the sacred beings less and associate with actual life more. When they explain some social phenomena, for example, love at first sight or parents bringing up children, they associate it with the sacred beings more and also they are difficult to separate themselves from the actual life. It means that people experience the supernatural reality less and interpret certain experience religiously more.

To make an analysis from ideology: To have the immortals in heart, people may think of themselves less. To believe in fate, people may think of other factors less. Most people, including some who identify themselves as religious, have other beliefs. Sometimes it is hard to see the differences on the surface but in their thoughts. The basic difference is that religious people explain something beyond actual life but the non religious people always explain something in regards to actual life. The second difference is that religious people not only have their beliefs but also have faith while non religious people have their beliefs but may have no faith. Faith is a strong belief which implies a feeling of respect for the beliefs. Because of the respect, people always try to defend their beliefs by behaviour. A pious religious believer always tries to keep in mind their beliefs and act it accordingly. A non religious believer does not have that feeling. His behaviour is diverse and changeable. The question is: how many people who have religious beliefs have faith as well nowadays?

In the theoretical part, some examples of human-immortal interaction were made according to some sociological theories. Roles of immortals were supposed according to those theories, for example, the immortals as significant others, the immortals in a frame forming. Practical survey of the dissertation shows that the immortals sometimes are significant others, it help people to build self concept and the immortals play a role in frame forming, it help people to interpret others.

4. Concept of Religion in People's Mind

In the theoretical part, some previous studies on the definition of religion were introduced, especially the ways of defining religion. An explicit definition of religion was not given at the beginning of the dissertation. However, a clear way of distinguishing people who are religious and who are not religious was stated. Those are people who believe or do not believe the existence of immortals in the beyond. In the interview outline, there is a question which asked people defining themselves as a religious or a non religious, and asked them to distinguish themselves from others. It aimed to know the concept of religion in people's mind. The term concept is used in the dissertation instead of the term definition. Concept is an idea underlying a class of things, a general notion (according to the definition in dictionary). Definition is a statement of a precisely meaning (according to the definition in dictionary). It is important to understand what people express and what are the meanings of their expression. In the interview outline, there is another question which asked people how they became a religious person or a non religious person and if they think that they may change their beliefs in the future. It aimed to know the process of a belief development.

4.1 Concept Having in People's Mind

The interview results according to the phrases which people used show that religion has two characteristics. It is a kind of belief, a belief in God, a belief in life after death, a belief in spirit, a belief in Karma. It is a kind of behaviour, to observe certain norms, to go to church, to practice meditation, to observe religious taboos. These two kinds of concepts are interrelated. Belief is the basis of religion. But only to say, for example, believe in God, the belief is in word. Behaviour is also important. But only behave in a certain way, for example, to go to the church, does not certainly mean religious. In addition, we have also social norms, non religious taboos. How can we make a distinction? Connecting the way by which to distinguish religious people and non religious people, it may say that anything which relate to the belief of the existence of immortals in the beyond can be regarded as religious otherwise it can be regarded as non religious. The concept has agreement with what the people expressed in the investigation.

The investigation results show that these concepts have impact on people's life, the beliefs in life and the way of living, how they interact with others, how they build relationship with others, how they deal with problems. The concepts have also impact on the human's culture. Lloyd Warner in "The Living and the Dead, A Study of the symbolic Life of Americans" says that human culture is inherited because the living generations have inherited form those now gone. "The human condition of individual mortality and the comparative immortality of our species make most of communication and collective activities in the larger sense a vast exchange of understanding between the living and the dead". "Thus, in fact, communication between the living and the dead individuals maintains continuity of culture for the species" (Warner 1959: pp.4-5).

4.2 Concept Building in People's Mind

The interview results according to the stories which people told about show that they became a religious by reading books, thinking a lot, school education, parents teaching, participating activities, and so on. In general, their religious concepts were built by both internal efforts and external influence. Some people who are not religious originally then became religious. Some people who are religious originally then they changed their religious beliefs. Talking about the future, some people's attitude is firm, they do not think that they will change their beliefs which they hold now. Some people's attitude is not firm, they do not know what they may believe in the future. It explains more or less that belief in some people's mind is uncertain, confusion and contradictory. The differences between what they hope in mind and what they see in reality make them fell confused. The differences between what they learned as a child and what they read and hear as an adult make them feel contradictory.

Charles Glock and Robert Bellah in "New Religious Consciousness" talk about the new religious consciousness from the angels of youth counterculture in 1960'. There are two kinds of consciousness in the past: individualistic mode and supernatural view. Then the third new consciousness emerged: "Its infirming power came from a way of comprehending the world basically at odds with individualistic and supernatural modes of consciousness" (Glock 1976: pp.356-366). The inspiration of his opinions is "If the past and present are any predictors of the future, there will be times again characterized by a lack of satisfaction with the everyday." "Being sure about the meaning of what is taking place is made difficult by the paucity of data. the snapshot afforded by the research undertaken to produce this volume is better than no data at all." "Simply stated, the thesis to be advanced and elaborated on is that the youth counterculture of the sixties was not the initiator of any significant change in American society. Rather, it will be argued that is was a highly visible sign of fundamental changes already under way."(Glock 1976: pp.353-355)

The forming of a concept or a belief needs a long process. It happens that a researcher makes a research only in a phase of the process. There were critical times or significant changes in history but that a research is made may not be just in time. Even if it is in time, the time of the research is limited. Researchers always hope that their results can show that "critical time" and "significant change". This may lead a research to a dangerous way because it may lead a research stress much some significant data but neglect anomalous data. The anomalous data, from a scientific view, is also a social reality, it may be or may have the potential to be critical and significant.

5. Conclusion

The topic of the dissertation "The Influence of Religious Beliefs on Social Interaction" focuses on religious beliefs in the existence of the immortals in the beyond and the social interaction among strangers and intimates. Both religious people and non religious people, both German persons and Chinese persons are included in the research in order to make a comparison possible. The basic assumptions in this dissertation are: 1) People who have religious beliefs may have something in common in social interaction. 2) People who have religious beliefs may behave differently in social interaction from people who do not have religious beliefs. 3) It is possible that the empirical facts contradict the first two assumptions. On the basis of the investigation and discussion, the conclusions can be summarized as follows:

People whose self ascribed identity defines them as religious, do have something in common. They have a common belief in the existence of immortals in the beyond. They believe that there is an intrapersonal relationship between this life and the next life and an interpersonal relationship between the living and the dead. Though the abstract concept of the immortal is clear, the concrete concept of the immortals' life is vague. God is a charismatic and powerful leader of the humans, to be more exact, a life consulter and director. God is a noble and prestigious model of the humans as well, to be more exact, a moral model and a fair judge. If we agree with the argument that the nature of the social relations determines the nature of the humans and the nature of the humans determines the nature of their imagery of the immortals, then the nature of God reflects the nature of the humans and the nature of humans reflects the social relations. The relation showing from this research is justice and harmony. No matter what the reality is, the religious belief is a voice from the people to their society.

The results from this research show that there are some people who expressed their uncertainty, confusion, or contradiction in beliefs. That is because everybody experiences two processes in life: one is his or her life cycle, the other is social change. It is possible that some people's beliefs change along with the changes of life events and social history. Some people also experienced a geographical social mobility, from one country to another country. This may bring them a lot of changes in religious orientation as well. The question can be asked: If a strong feeling of respect for the beliefs (a faith) motivates people to defend their beliefs by behaviour, how many people whose self identities are religious have such strong feeling nowadays?

People who have religious beliefs are supposed to have common characteristics in social interaction. It is true that people who have religious beliefs have something in common but the common characters are not very significant for this research because people who have religious beliefs and people who do not have religious beliefs behave in a similar way when they interact with strangers and with their intimates. The differences do not reflect on the people's behaviour but on the people's motives for the behaviour and attribution style. Behind the overt behaviour, it embodies the motives of associating with strangers and the intimates in order to "win the honour for God" or "win favour of God". Behind the overt behaviour of dealing with problems, it embodies the attribution style "to attribute problems to fate". Because of the attribution, some of the religious believers pray to God, the powerful being of destiny, for help. Of course, God is not the only goal to reach, fate is not the only factors to attribute. That is why the results on the aspect of interaction from this research are not the same as it is supposed. The reality tells us that religious beliefs do have influence on social interaction but the influence of religious belief is not the only factor to influence people.

In the results of the research, there is a typical word which is repeated by some people when they talked about associating with strangers "It depends". It depends on the situation of the interaction. It depends on the both sides of the interaction. It indicates that interaction between people is a complex process: sending words and cues and receiving and processing words and cues as they come in from the other side. It also indicates that people negotiate which roles they are going to play in a situation. In the results of the research, another typical word which is repeated by some people is "In between" (between the two extreme points). When they talked about associating with the intimates, it is regarded as a skill of communication from the view of the people. It is also a principle of behaviour from the view of the research, a principle of appropriateness, not to go too far to control, not to go too near to reach the goal. An open question is: In what situation do people behave as much as they like heartily or enjoy themselves thoroughly?

Comparing the differences between the religious believers and non religious believers, the differences between the Germans and the Chinese is interesting. The focus is on the concept of ancestor worship. Ancestor worship is a tradition with a long history in Asia. It resulted from secular feelings of love for the dead relatives. This tradition still has its influence in some Chinese people's mind. To be grateful to the ancestors, to pray to the ancestors for protection and to show filial piety to the ancestors leads to the result that Chinese people pay more attention to the family and children, to their blood relationship. The basic data from the questionnaire show that the percentage of the people who get married among the Chinese are higher than among the Germans and the percentage of the people who have children are also higher among the Chinese than among the Germans. Though people may not express their real motives of building a family or having children directly, the traditional concept may still have influence in many people's mind.

The results from the research show that the involvement of the heart is the condition of beliefs taking effect. If somebody believes something without the heart being involved, the belief is only in word. The belief will not be efficacious. It is only possible that the immortals are present when somebody's heart is there. If somebody says something to the immortals with his or her heart, the immortals also listen attentively. If somebody says something to the immortals without the heart, the immortals also listen carelessly. If somebody meets the immortals with the heart, the immortal will have a big influence on the person. Sometimes the immortals may become the "significant other" to influence the person's self concept. Sometimes the immortals may play a role in one's "frame" forming (E. Goffman) to influence one's interpretation in a situation. The question arises: If a sincere heart is the condition for beliefs to take effect, what will be the result of half-believing and half-doubting?

Going to the last issue of the dissertation, also the basic issue of the research, what is the concept of religion? In the theoretical part of the dissertation it could be shown that previous research involved both: how to define religion (what religion is) and how to approach religion (what religion does). How do we define religion? Religion is a belief in the existence of immortals in the beyond. Religion is an experience of the interaction with immortals in the beyond. Religion is a behaviour to present the beliefs and the experience. Religion is a system of making the religious beliefs and behaviour into an organic whole. How do we approach religion? It can be approached as an interaction in the form of the human-immortal communication, for example, to approach that people communicate immortals with heart. It can be approached as an interpretation of social phenomena as reality in a sacred cosmos, for example, to approach that people interpret life events by fate. It can be approached as an influential factor having influence on social interaction, for example, the role religious beliefs play in social interaction. It can be approached as a compensating and comforting illusion to fulfil the humans needs, for example, that people feel satisfied after they pray. It can be approached as cognition of human development and social change, for example, that the concept of religion develops. The research results show that the concept of religion in people's mind is divergent and the concept of religion in some people's mind is uncertainty, confusion or contradiction. The forming of a concept or a belief needs a long process. A researcher makes a research only in a very short phase of the process. There are many critical times or significant changes in history but that research is carried out may not happen just in time. But if we keep on using our own eyes to observe the world, the critical time or significant change may come in the near future.

End

München, October 8, 2003

Reference

Aldridge, Alan (2000), *Religion in the Contemporary World: A Sociological Introduction*, Malden: Polity Press in association with Blackwell

Atkinson, Rita L., Richard C. Atkinson, Edward E. Smith, Daryl J. Bem, and Susan Nolen-Hoeksema (1993), *Introduction to Psychology*, 11th Edition, Fort Worth: Harcourt Brace College Publishers

Berger, Peter L. (1969), *The Social Reality of Religion*, London: Faber and Faber

Berger, Peter L. and Thomas Luckmann (1973), *The Social Construction of Reality*, Harmondsworth: Penguin

Coward, Harold (1997), *Life after Death in World Religion*, New York: Orbis Books

Glock, Charles Y. and Robert N. Bellah (1976), *The New Religious Consciousness*, Los Angeles: University of California Press

Goffman, Erving (1974), *Frame Analysis, An Essay on the Organization of Experience*, Massachusetts: Harvard University Press

Hamilton, Malcolm B. (1995), *The Sociology of Religion, Theoretical and Comparative Perspectives*, London: Routledge

Haralambos, Michael and Martin Holborn (1990), *Sociology Themes and Perspectives*, 3th edition, London: Unwin Hyman

Helle, Horst & Ludwig Nieder (1997), *Georg Simmel, Essays on Religion*, New Haven: Yale University Press

Helle, Horst *Erving Goffman: A Symbolic Interactionist?*, Tomasi, Luigi (1998), *The Tradition of the Chicago School of Sociology*, England: Ashgate

Helle, Horst (2001), *Georg Simmel: Introduction to his Theory and Method*, Muenchen: Oldenbourg

Johnstone, Ronald L. (1997), *Religion in Society: A Sociology of Religion*, 5th edition, New Jersey: Prentice-Hall

Kammeger, Kenneth C., George Ritzer, and Norman R. Yetman (1997), *Sociology, Experiencing Changing Societies*, 7th edition, Boston: Allyn and Bacon

Karp, David A. (1986), *Sociology and Everyday Life*, Itasca: Peacock Publisher

Mead, George H. (1967), *Mind, Self, and Society, From The Standpoint of A Social Behaviorist*, Chicago: The University of Chicago Press

Neuman, W. Lawrence (1994); *Social Research Methods: Qualitative and Quantitative Approaches*, 2th Edition, Needham Heights: Allyn and Bacon

Peterson, Michael, William Hasker, Bruce Reichenbach, and David Basinger (1998), *Reason & Religious Belief*, 2th edition, New York: Oxford University Press

Prager, Karen J. (1995), *The Psychology of Intimacy*, New York: Guilford Press

Ritzer, George (1992), *Sociological Theory*, 3th edition, New York: McGraw-Hill

Tashakkori, Abbas and Teddlie, Charles (1998), *Mixed Methodology, Combining Qualitative and Quantitative Approaches*, Thousand Oaks: Sage Publication

Turner, Jonathan H. (1991), *The Structure of Sociological Theory*, 5th edition, Belmont: Wadsworth

Wall, George B. (1995), *Religious Experience and Religious Belief*, Boston: Univesity Press of America

Warner, W. Lloyd (1959), *The Living and the Dead, A Study of the Symbolic Life of Americans*, New Haven: Yale University Press

Weiner, Bernard (1980), *Human Motivation*, New York: Holt, Rinehart and Winston

韩明谟, 王思斌:社会学概论, 中央广播电视大学出版社, 北京 1993 年

侯杰, 范丽珠:中国民众宗教意识, 天津人民出版社, 天津 1994 年

吕大吉:宗教学通论新编, 中国社会科学出版社, 北京 1998 年

牟钟鉴, 张践:中国宗教通史, 社会科学文献出 版 社, 北京 2000 年
沈德灿:社会心理学, 中国科学技术出版社, 北京 1995 年
袁方, 王汉生:社会研究方法教程, 北京大学出版社, 北京 1997 年

Appendix 1

Questionnaire: Beliefs and Behavior in Everyday Life
December, 2002

Dear Madam, Dear Sir:
We are researchers of the Institute of Sociology, Munich University. Your answers to these questions will help us to learn more about what people believe and how people behave in everyday life. You need not write your name on the questionnaire and we will keep the data secret. Thank you very much for your cooperation!

Direction:

1. Please read each question and circle the number that best indicates what you agree with.
2. You just need to choose one answer to each of the questions.
3. If the given answers are not suitable for you, you circle the answer "other" and explain it.
4. Your answers will not be judged as right or wrong. Your opinion counts.

Personal Data:

1. Sex: (1) male________ (2) female________

2. Age: ________

3. Marriage: (1) single________ (2) married________ (3) divorced________ (4) widowed________

4. Education: (1) no university education________ (2) have university education________

5. Occupation: please write __________

6. Income: (1) insufficient________ (2) sufficient________ (3) surplus________

7. Children: (1) no________ (2) have (number?) ________

8. Partner: (1) education __________ (2) occupation __________

9. Country of Origin: please write__________

10. Religious Belief: please write__________

Your Answers (choose a number):

1. If a stranger helps you on his own initiative in a place which you do not know
   (1) You will be happy and accept it.
   (2) You will be upset and refuse it.
   (3) Others (explain it):
2. If a newcomer joins your work or study group
   (1) You will be close to him and let him know you.
   (2) You will keep a distance to him and observe what he is.
   (3) Other (explain it):
3. If you go to a new place to work or study without a person whom you know
   (1) You will be close to others and try to know others.
   (2) You will keep a distance to others and maintain your anonymity.
   (3) Other (explain it):
4. If a newcomer makes a suggestion on your work
   (1) You will be thankful and consider it.
   (2) You will be annoyed and ignore it.
   (3) Other (explain):
5. to contact with your partner
   (1) You often tell him or her your private thoughts.
   (2) You often hide your private thoughts from him or her.
   (3) Other (explain it):
6. to contact with your partner
   (1) You often express your feelings to him or her.
   (2) You often control your feelings to him or her.
   (3) Other (explain it):
7. to contact with your partner
   (1) You are interested in what he or she is interested.

(2) You have your interests and he or she has his or hers.

(3) Other (explain it):

8. to contact with your partner

(1) You always try to understand him or her as much as you can.

(2) You need not understand him or her that much.

(3) Other (explain it):

9. If a man and a woman fall in love at first sight

(1) It is because of fate.

(2) It is because that they find each other congenial.

(3) Other (explain it):

10. Two persons feel like old friends at the first meeting

(1) It is because of fate.

(2) It is because that they find each other congenial.

(3) Other (explain it):

11. Parents bring up children

(1) In order to have people remember them forever.

(2) In order to ask them to provide for the aged.

(3) In order to have the human beings multiply.

(4) Other (explain it):

12. Parents expect children to become useful persons

(1) In order to bring honour to the family.

(2) In order to make children independent.

(3) In order to contribute to the society.

(4) Other (explain it):

13. What does it mean when your body is dead?

(1) It means that my life experienced a turning point.

(2) It means that my life is finished forever.

(3) Other (explain it):

14. Where will you go after your body is dead?

(1) I will go to another place to live in another form.

(2) I will go to the graveyard to sleep under the ground.

(3) Other (explain it):

15. What do you think about your dead relatives?

(1) They are still living somewhere.

(2) They disappeared from this world.

(3) Other (explain it):

16. Sometimes your dead relatives may appear in front of you

(1) It is a reality, they really come to me.

(2) It is a fantasy that I just think of them.

(3) Other (explain it):

17. Everyone has a lot of things to deal with and a lot of desires to fulfill

(1) Life is eternal. If one cannot do what he wants in this life, he can do it in the next life.

(2) Life is limited. If one cannot do what he wants in this life, he will not have opportunities later.

(3) Other (explain it):

18. Everyone may do a lot of good things or bad things this life

(1) One will receive the reward or punishment in the next life.

(2) One will not be bound anymore after one finishes his life.

(3) Other (explain it):

19. Our ancestors or god gave us life and created the world

(1) They have power to dominate and manipulate us in this world.

(2) They have no power because they are gone or never existed.

(3) Other (explain it)

20. Our descendants will live in this world after we leave here

(1) They are the extension of my life because the blood in their vessel is the same as mine.

(2) They are the successors to my cause because thy can continue working after I die.

(3) Other (explain it):

21. When you suffer setbacks in everyday life

(1) You usually find ways to solve the problems.

(2) You usually comfort yourself not to think about it.

(3) You usually pray.

(4) Other (explain it):

22. You may face many obstacles in everyday life

(1) Most of them result from your own factors.

(2) Most of them result from external factors.

(3) Most of them are decreed by fate.

(4) Other (explain it):

23. Sometimes when I do something

(1) I feel that my ancestors or god are watching me.

(2) I feel that other people are watching me.

(3) Both (1) and (2), (4) Other (explain it):

24. When I do something, I pay more attention to

(1) Others' evaluation

(2) My own experience

(3) Both (1) and (2), (4) Other (explain it):

Appendix 2

Interview Outline

Beliefs and Behavior in Everyday Life

December, 2002

1. Being a stranger in a place which you do not know
   How do you usually associate with others at the beginning?
   Why? Examples?
2. To see a stranger in a place which you are familiar
   How do you usually associate with him or her at the beginning?
   Why? Examples?
3. To contact with your partner or the intimates
   Do you often tell him or her about your private thoughts?
   Do you often express your feelings to him or her?
   Why?
4. To contact with your partner or the intimates
   Can you share interests with him or her?
   Can you understand him or her as much as you can?
   Why?
5. If a man and a woman fall in love at first sight
   or divorce after living together for many years
   How do you explain it?
   Examples?
6. Two persons feel like old friends at the first meeting
   or know for a long time but fight each other often
   How do you explain it?
   Examples?

7. For what purposes do parents bring up children?
   Is it important for one to have children ?
8. Why do parents expect children to become useful persons?
   Is it meaningful for the parents themselves?
9. What do you usually do when you suffer setbacks?
   Examples?
10. What do the obstacles result from in your life?
    Examples?
11. What does it mean when your body is dead?
    Why?
12. Where will you go after your body is dead?
    Why?
13. Is a person's life eternal or limited?
    Why?
14. Is there a relationship between what one does now and hereafter?
    Why?
15. What do you think about your dead relatives?
    Are they still living somewhere?
    Did they disappear from this world?
    Why?
16. Is it a reality or a fantasy if your dead relatives appear in front of you?
    Do they really come to you?
    Do you just think of them?
    Why?
17. Our ancestors or god (if you believe) gave us life and created the world
    Do they have power to dominate and manipulate us in this world?
    Why?
18. Our descendants will live in this world after we leave here
    What is the meaning of that? Why?

19. Sometimes when you do something,

Do you feel that your ancestors or god are watching you?

Do you feel that that other people are watching you?

Examples?

20. When you do something,

Do you pay more attention to others' evaluation?

Do you pay more attention to your own experience?

Examples?

21. Do you think that you are a religious person?

How do you distinguish yourself from others?

How did you become a religious person?

Do you think that you may become one in the future?

Peter Lang · Europäischer Verlag der Wissenschaften

Doris Weiss (ed.)

Social Exclusion

An Approach to the Australian Case

Frankfurt am Main, Berlin, Bern, Bruxelles, New York, Oxford, Wien, 2003.
423 pp., 3 fig., 2 tab.
ISBN 3-631-51084-5 / US-ISBN 0-8204-6454-6 · pb. € 68.50*

Far and away from the academic world with its theoretical discussion of what is meant by social exclusion and the empirical attempts to measure it, is the painful reality that confronts large portions of society on a daily basis. This book represents a contribution to the discussion on social exclusion in politics and social sciences. However, beyond this, it is the social reality in Australia that this work hopes to address.

Contents: Immigration · Multiculturalism · Chinese and Italian and German Migration · Second Generation · Citizenship · Access and Equity · Cultural Politics and Children · Welfare State · Labour market · Inequality and Social Class · Situation of Aboriginals · Gender · Artists · Gay and Lesbian people

Frankfurt am Main · Berlin · Bern · Bruxelles · New York · Oxford · Wien
Distribution: Verlag Peter Lang AG
Moosstr. 1, CH-2542 Pieterlen
Telefax 00 41 (0) 32 / 376 17 27

*The €-price includes German tax rate
Prices are subject to change without notice

Homepage http://www.peterlang.de

FSC
www.fsc.org
MIX
Papier | Fördert gute Waldnutzung
FSC® C083411

Kolibri 360 GmbH
Ferdinand-Jühlke-Straße 7
99095 Erfurt, Deutschland
produktsicherheit@kolibri360.de

Druck:
CPI Druckdienstleistungen GmbH
im Auftrag der
Kolibri 360 GmbH
Ferdinand-Jühlke-Str. 7
99095 Erfurt